U.S. EDITION

PRIMARY MATHEMATICS 1B

TEXTBOOK

Marshall Cavendish Education

SingaporeMath.com Inc

Original edition published under the title Primary Mathematics Textbook 1B

© 1981 Curriculum Planning & Development Division

Ministry of Education, Singapore

Published by Times Media Private Limited

This American Edition

© 2003 Times Media Private Limited

© 2003 Marshall Cavendish International (Singapore) Private Limited

Published by Marshall Cavendish Education

An imprint of Marshall Cavendish International (Singapore) Private Limited

A member of Times Publishing Limited

Times Centre, 1 New Industrial Road, Singapore 536196

Customer Service Hotline: (65) 6411 0820

E-mail: fps@sg.marshallcavendish.com

Website: www.marshallcavendish.com/education/sg

Distributed by

SingaporeMath.com Inc

404 Beavercreek Road #225

Oregon City, OR 97045

U.S.A.

Website: http://www.singaporemath.com

First published 2003

Reprinted 2003, 2004 (twice)

Second impression 2005

Reprinted 2005, 2006 (twice), 2007, 2008, 2009

ISBN 978-981-01-8495-7

Printed in Singapore by Times Graphics Pte Ltd

ACKNOWLEDGEMENTS

Our special thanks to Richard Askey, Professor of Mathematics (University of Wisconsin, Madison), Yoram Sagher, Professor of Mathematics (University of Illinois, Chicago), and Madge Goldman, President (Gabriella and Paul Rosenbaum Foundation), for their indispensable advice and suggestions in the production of Primary Mathematics (U.S. Edition).

PREFACE

Primary Mathematics (U.S. Edition) comprises textbooks and workbooks. The main feature of this package is the use of the **Concrete → Pictorial → Abstract** approach. The students are provided with the necessary learning experiences beginning with the concrete and pictorial stages, followed by the abstract stage to enable them to learn mathematics meaningfully. This package encourages active thinking processes, communication of mathematical ideas and problem solving.

The textbook comprises 9 units. Each unit is divided into parts: ❶, ❷, . . . Each part starts with a meaningful situation for communication and is followed by specific learning tasks numbered 1, 2, . . . The textbook is accompanied by a workbook. The sign Workbook Exercise is used to link the textbook to the workbook exercises.

Practice exercises are designed to provide the students with further practice after they have done the relevant workbook exercises. Review exercises are provided for cumulative reviews of concepts and skills. All the practice exercises and review exercises are optional exercises.

The color patch ■ is used to invite active participation from the students and to facilitate oral discussion. The students are advised not to write on the color patches.

CONTENTS

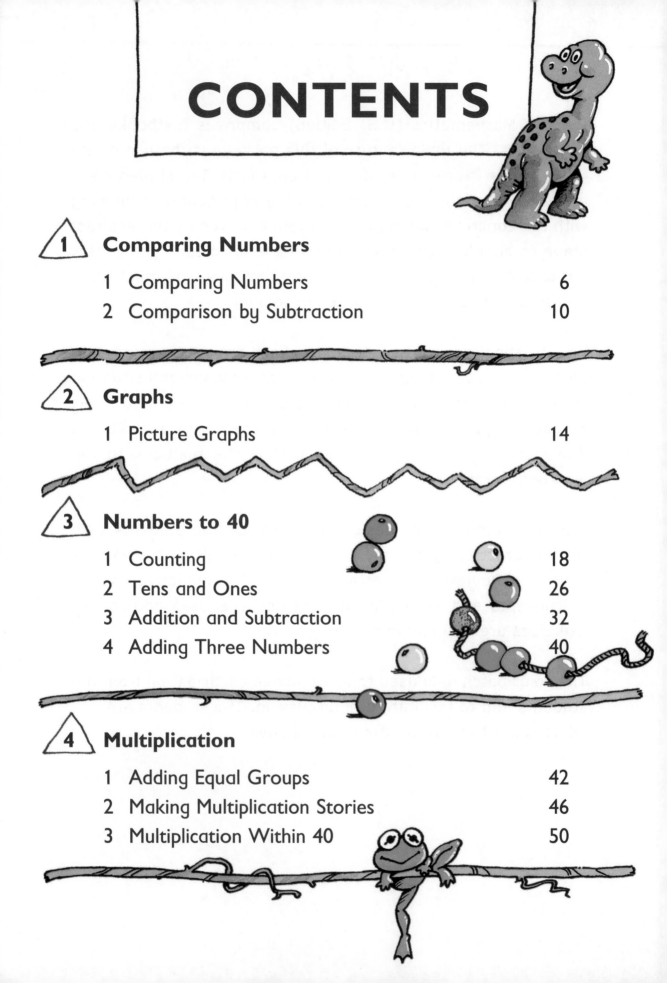

$15

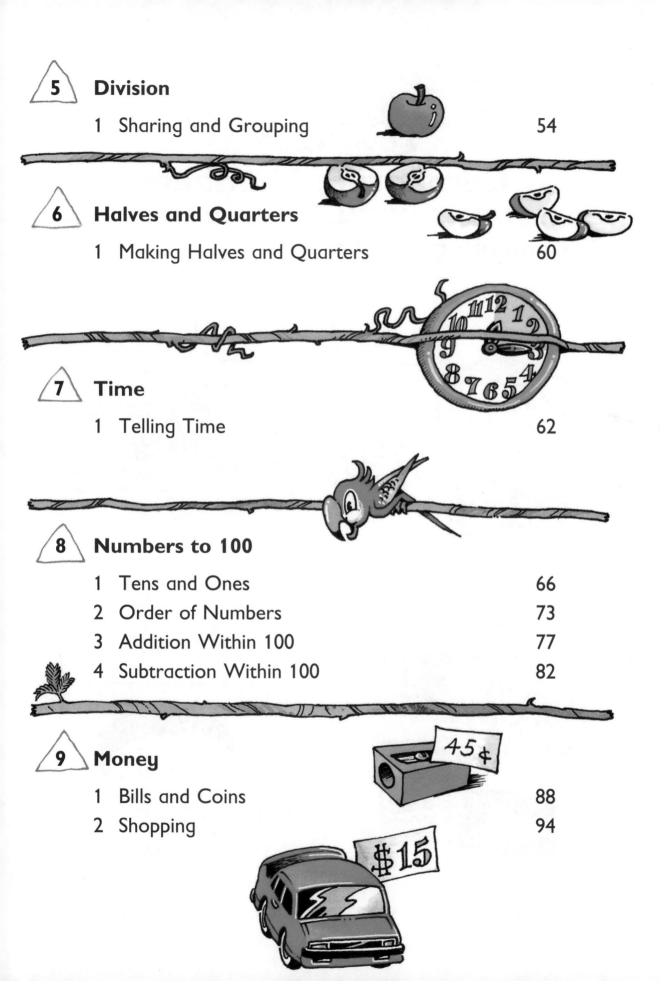

1 Comparing Numbers

1 Comparing Numbers

I have 3 stamps.
Matthew

I have 4 stamps.
John

Who has more stamps, Matthew or John?

1. Are there more frogs than penguins?

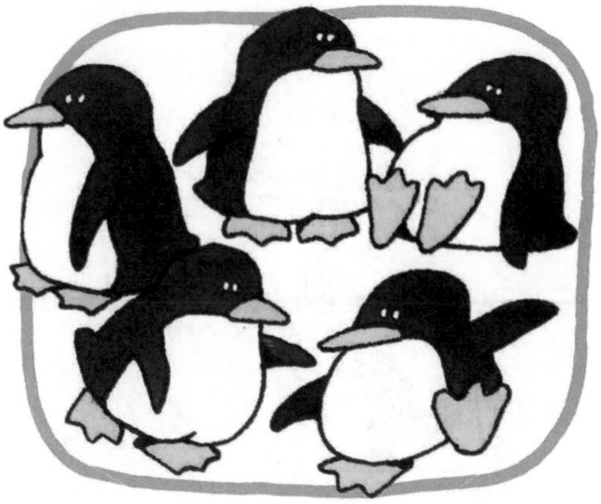

2. Are there more carrots than rabbits?

3. Are there more mangoes than pineapples?

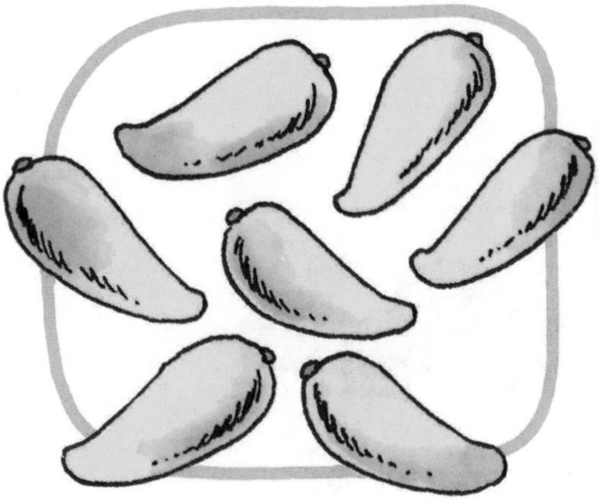

Workbook Exercise 1

4. (a) Which set has more stamps?

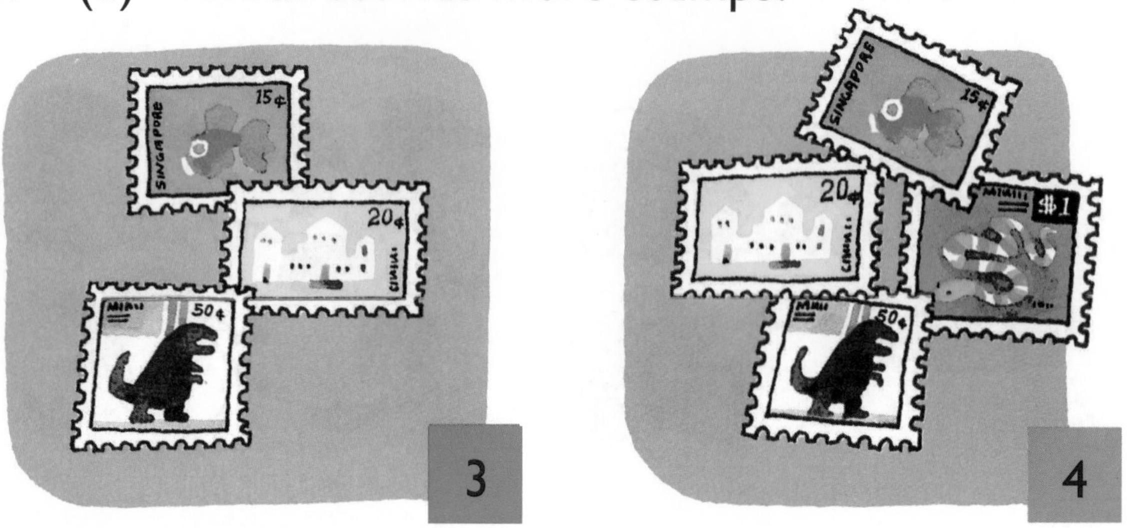

(b) What number is 1 **more** than 3?

5.

What number is 1 more than 8?

6. (a) What number is 1 more than 5?

(b) What number is 1 more than 6?

7. (a) What number is 1 **less** than 7?

(b) What number is 1 less than 6?

8.

What number is 1 less than 10?

9. (a) What number is 1 more than 7?

(b) What number is 1 less than 9?

2 Comparison by Subtraction

There are 3 more flowers than butterflies.

There are 3 fewer butterflies than flowers.

We can compare two numbers by subtraction.
5 – 2 = 3

1. Write a number sentence for each story.

(a)

5 - 3 = 2

There are 2 more rabbits than carrots.

(b)

Juan has ☐ fewer robots than Peter.

(c)

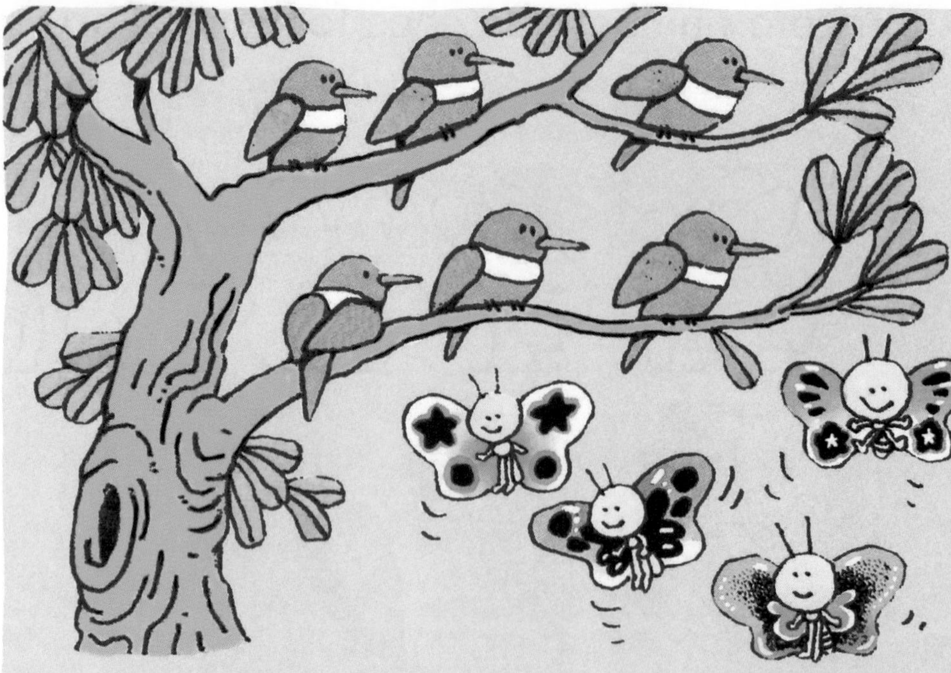

There are ☐ fewer butterflies than birds.

(d)

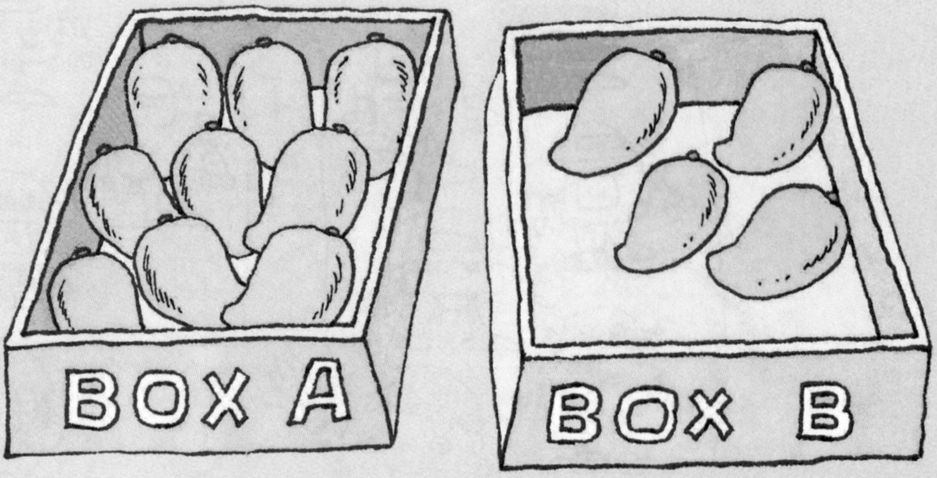

There are ☐ more mangoes in Box A than in Box B.

(e)

Amy has ☐ more dolls than robots.

(f)

Sam buys ☐ fewer pineapples than mangoes.

Workbook Exercises 3 to 6

2

Graphs

1 Picture Graphs

Place a color chip on each toy.

Use the same color for each type of toy.

Then make a picture graph like this:

The picture graph shows the number of each type of toy.

How many balls are there?

How many more cars than dolls are there?

How many fewer cars than balls are there?

How many toys are there altogether?

1.

(a) ▭ children have their birthdays in July.

(b) ▭ more children have their birthdays in July than in May.

2. Ali, Rahim and Rosni like to read books.
This picture graph shows the number of books they read last week.

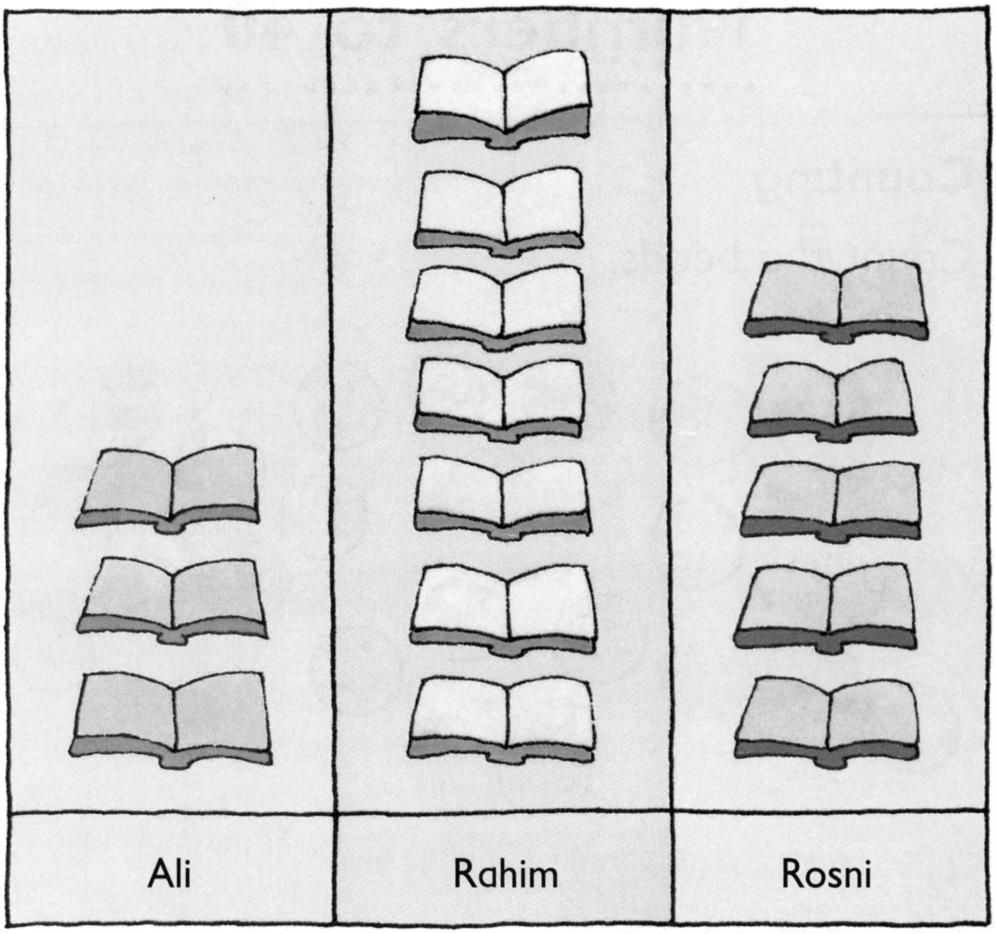

(a) Ali read ☐ books.

(b) ☐ read the most books.

(c) Rosni read ☐ more books than Ali.

(d) They read ☐ books altogether.

Workbook Exercises 7 to 9

3

Numbers to 40

1 Counting

Count the beads.

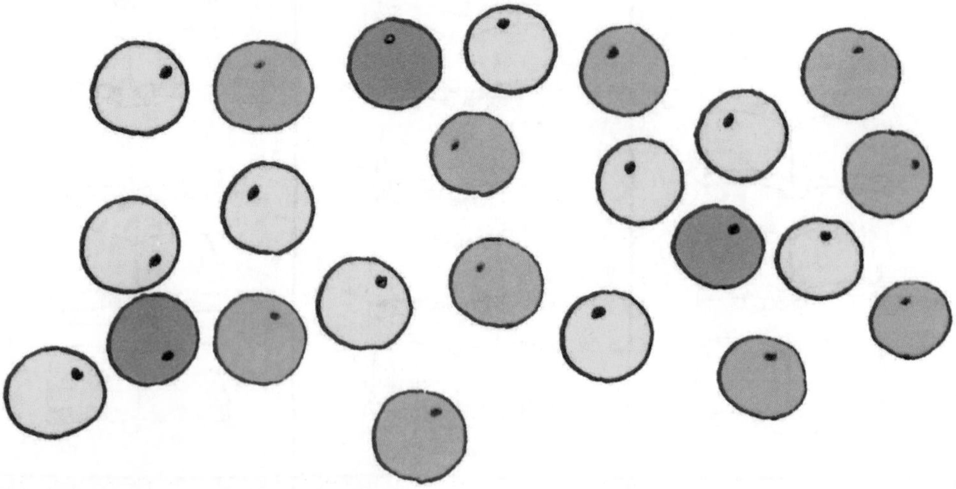

There are more than 20 beads.
1, 2, 3, 4, 5, 6, 7, 8, 9, 10, 11, 12, 13, 14, 15, 16, 17, 18, 19, 20, . . .

Make tens and count.

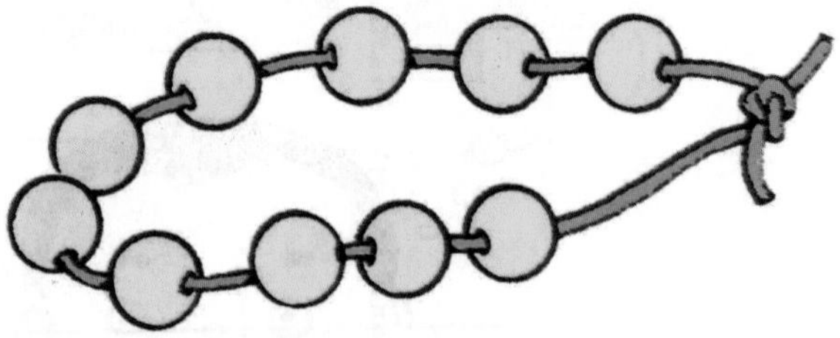

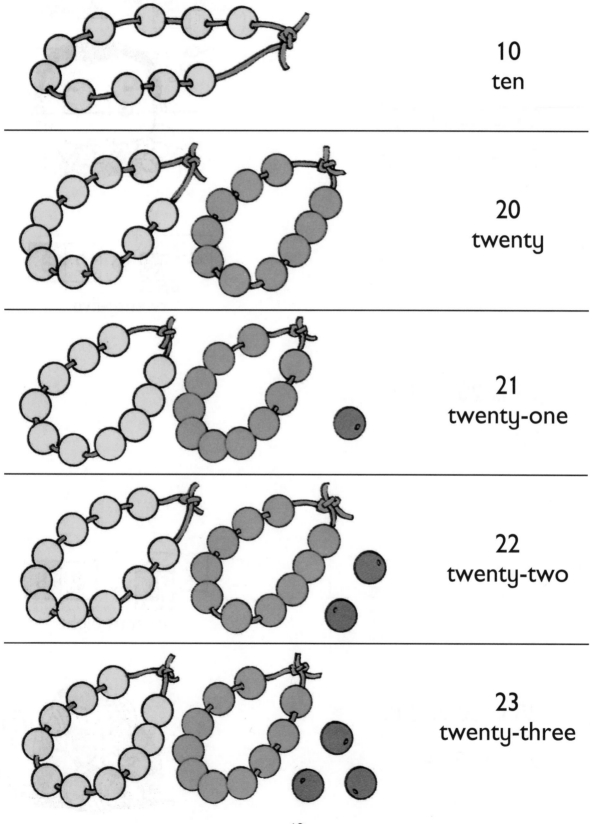

10
ten

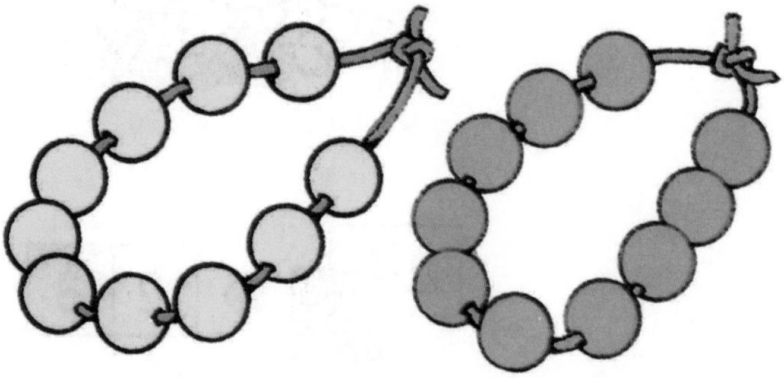

20
twenty

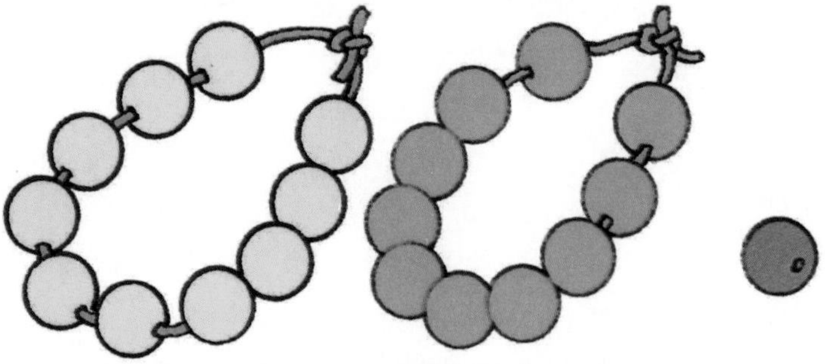

21
twenty-one

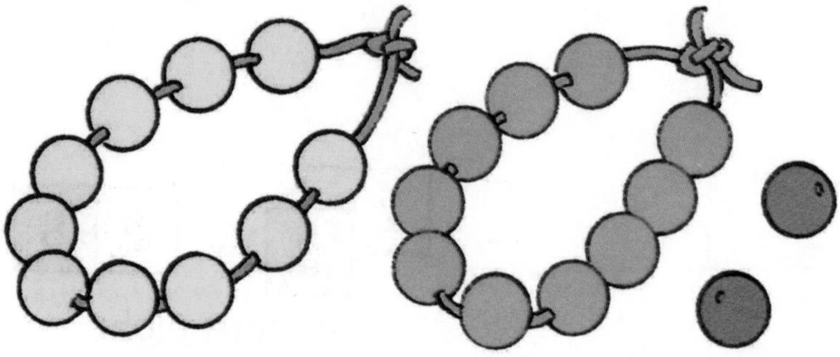

22
twenty-two

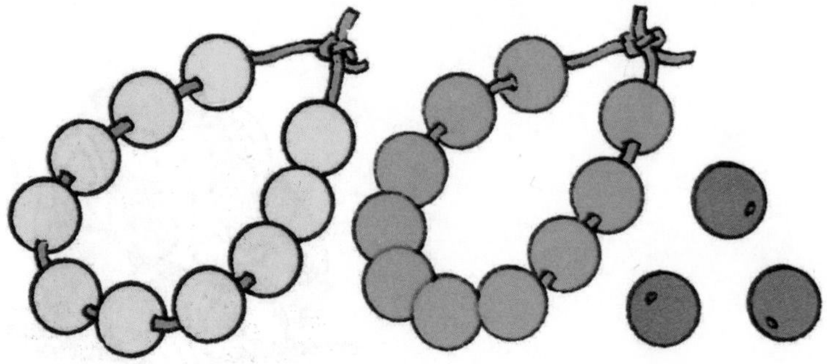

23
twenty-three

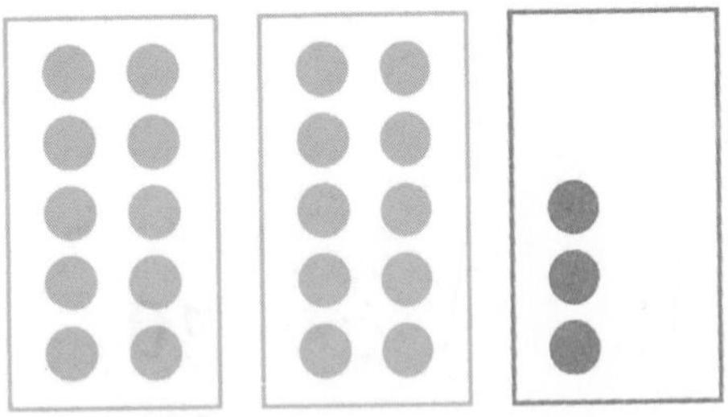

23 is 20 and 3.

20 + 3 = 23

1. 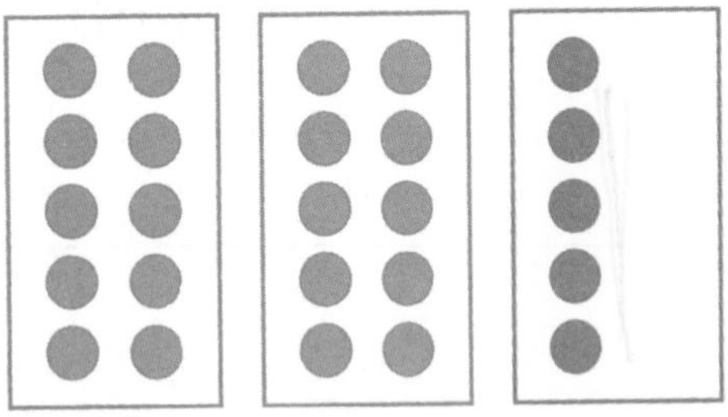

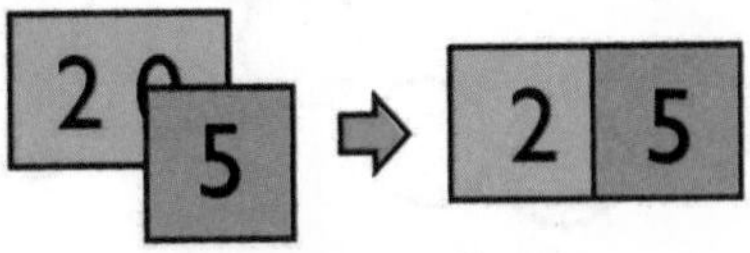

twenty-five

25 is 20 and 5.

20 + 5 = 25

2. 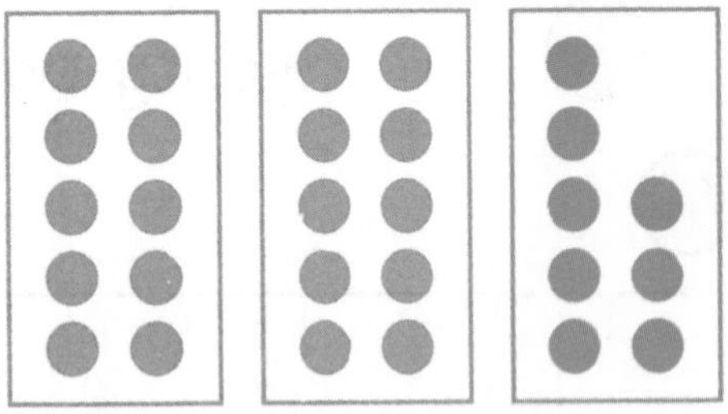

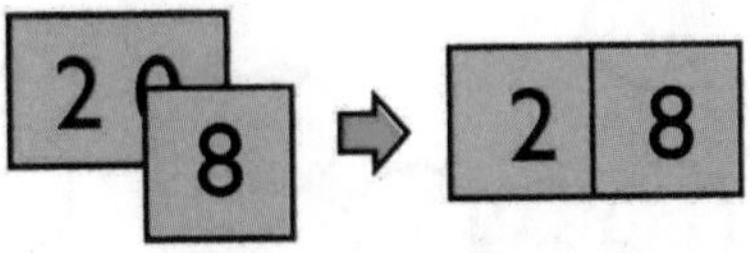

twenty-eight

28 is 20 and 8.

20 + 8 = 28

1	2	3	4	5	6	7	8	9	10
11	12	13	14	15	16	17	18	19	20
21	22	23	24	25	26	27	28	29	30
31	32	33	34	35	36	37	38	39	40

3. 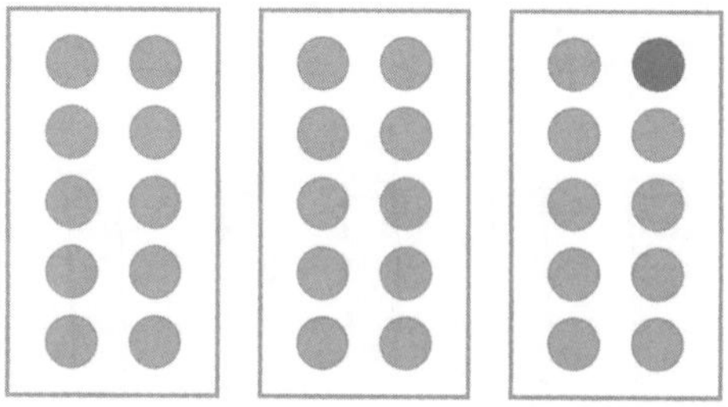

29 and 1 make 30.

29 + 1 = ☐

4. 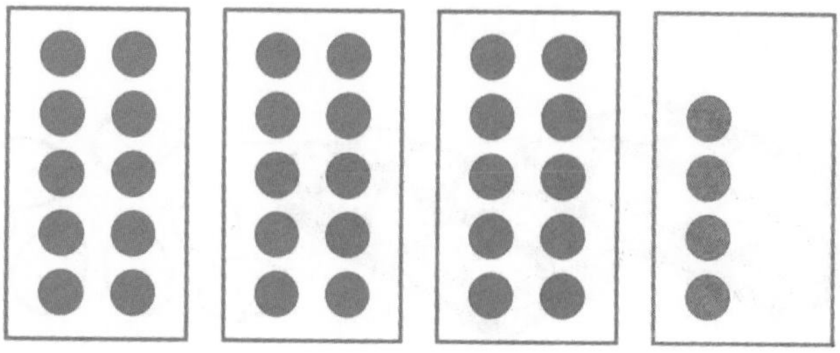

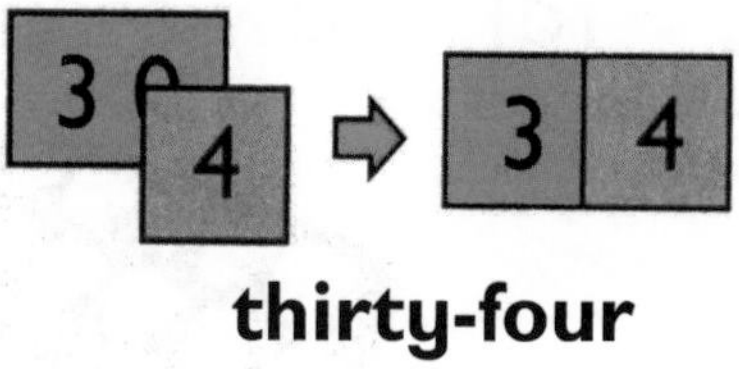

30 and 4 make 34.

30 + 4 = 34

5.

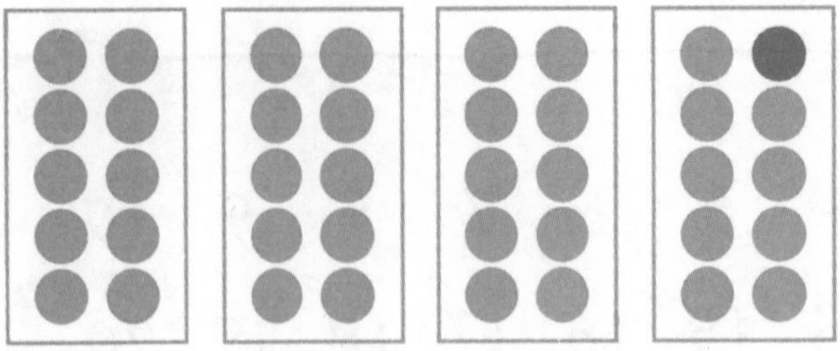

40
forty

1 more than 39 is 40.

39 + 1 = 40

Workbook Exercise 10 & 11

6. (a) How many sticks are there?

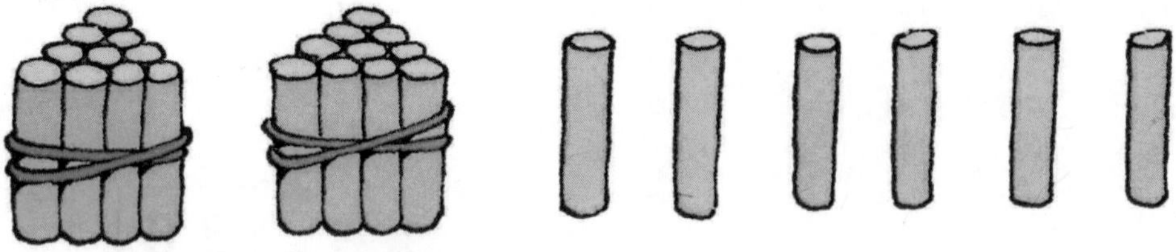

(b) 20 + 6 = 26

(c) 6 more than 20 is 26.

7. (a) How many eggs are there?

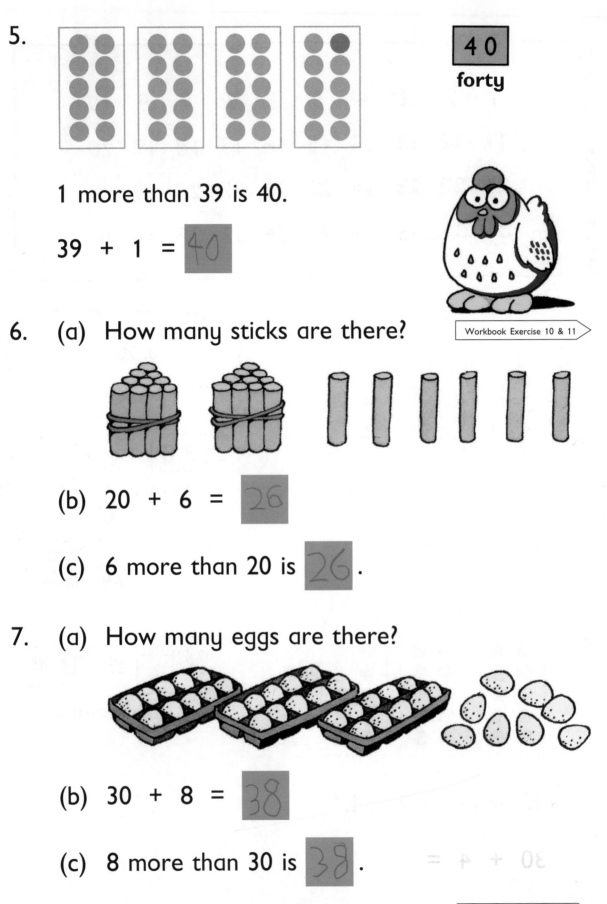

(b) 30 + 8 = 38

(c) 8 more than 30 is 38.

Workbook Exercise 12

8. (a)

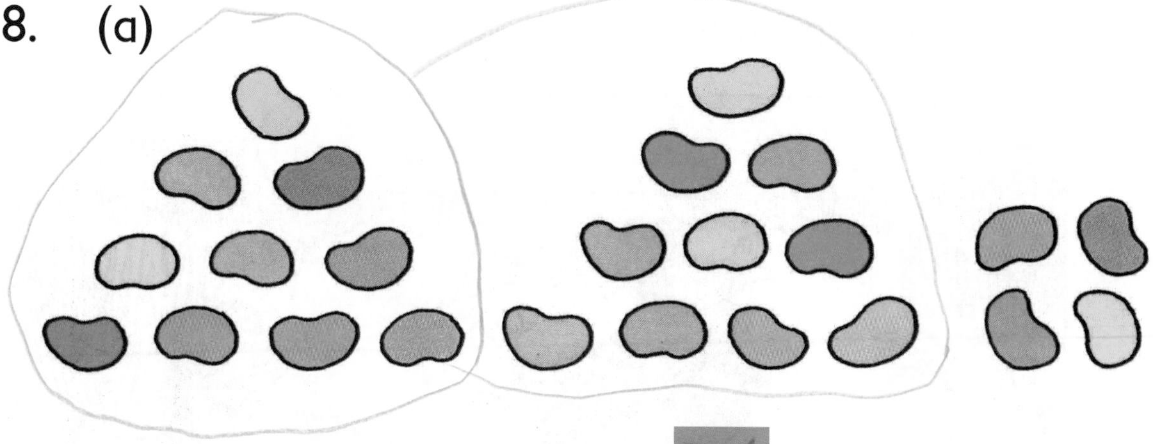

$20 + 4 = 24$

(b)

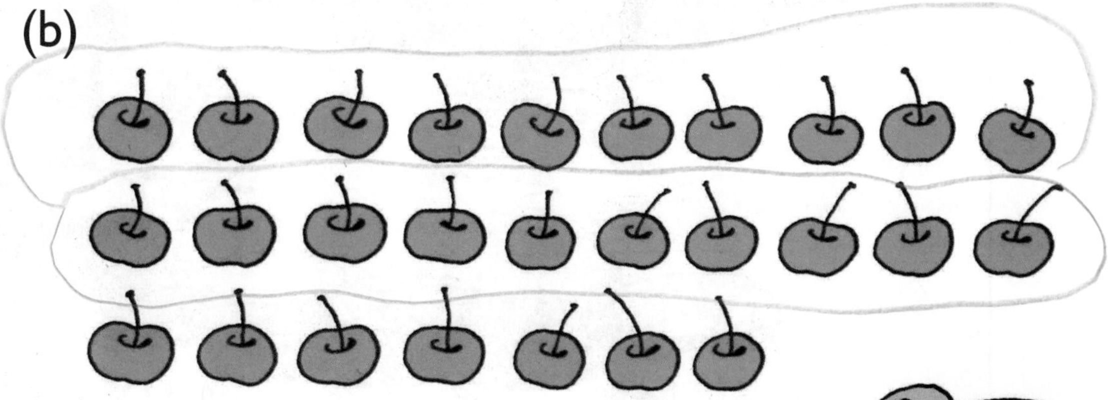

$20 + 7 = 27$

(c)

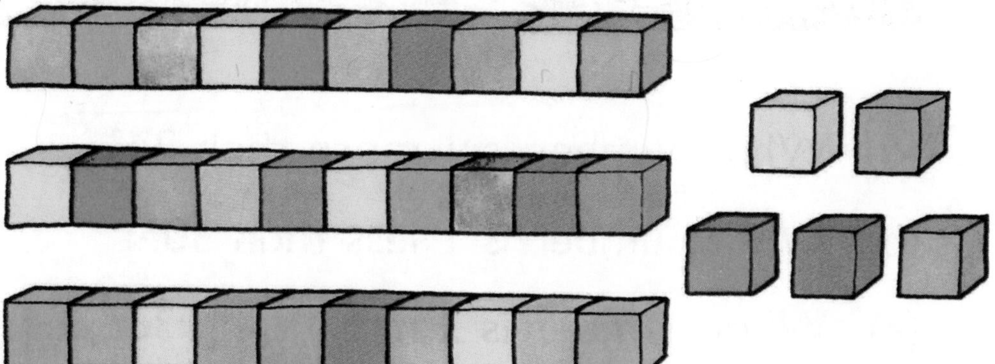

$30 + 5 = 35$

9. What are the missing numbers?

10. (a) What number is 1 more than 24? — 25

(b) What number is 1 less than 30? — 29

(c) What number is 2 more than 36? — 38

(d) What number is 2 less than 28? — 26

11. (a) Which is greater, 24 or 27?

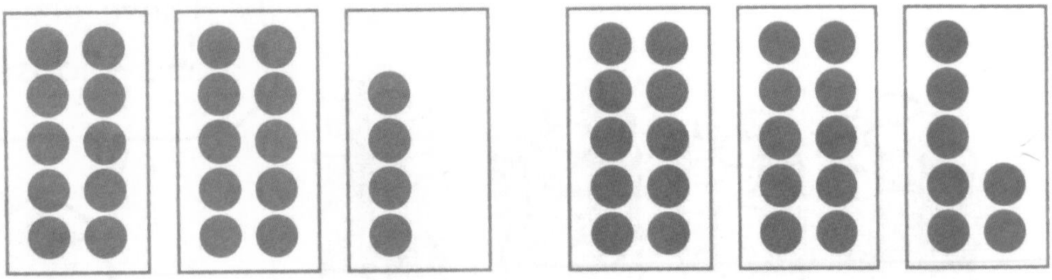

(b) Which is smaller, 36 or 38?

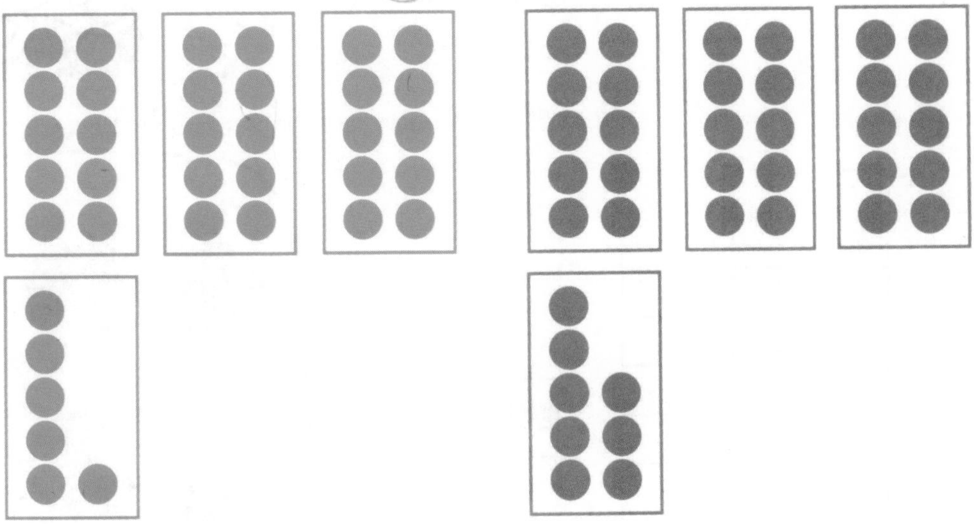

12. Compare these numbers.

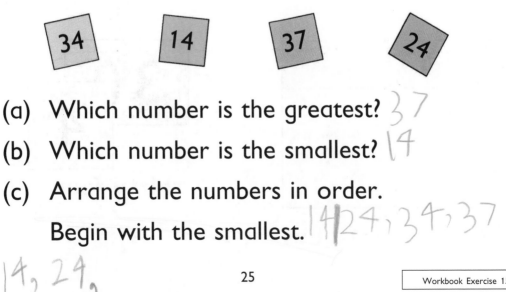

(a) Which number is the greatest? 37

(b) Which number is the smallest? 14

(c) Arrange the numbers in order.

Begin with the smallest. 14, 24, 34, 37

14, 24,

2 Tens and Ones

There are 3 tens
and 4 loose ones.

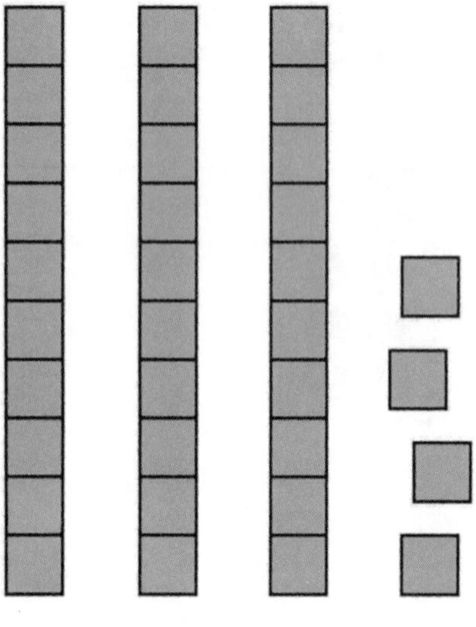

Tens	Ones
3	4

34 = 3 tens 4 ones

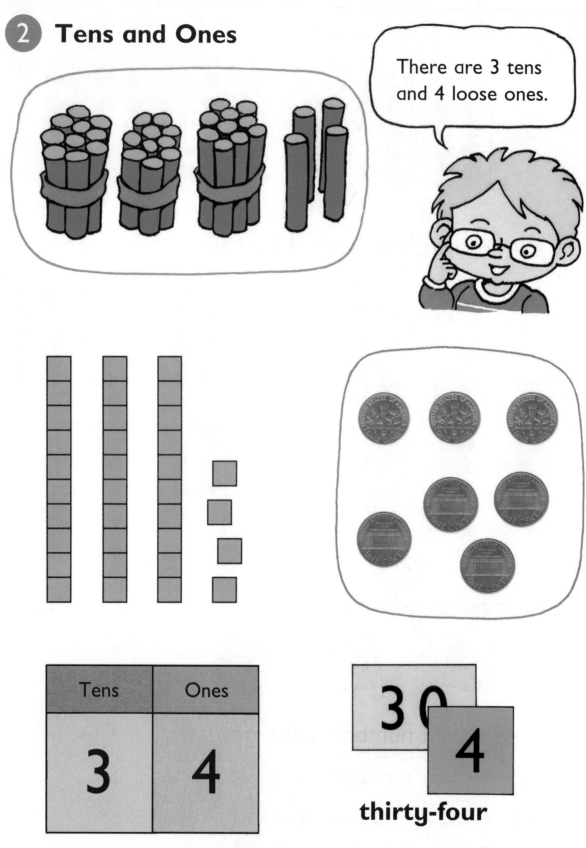

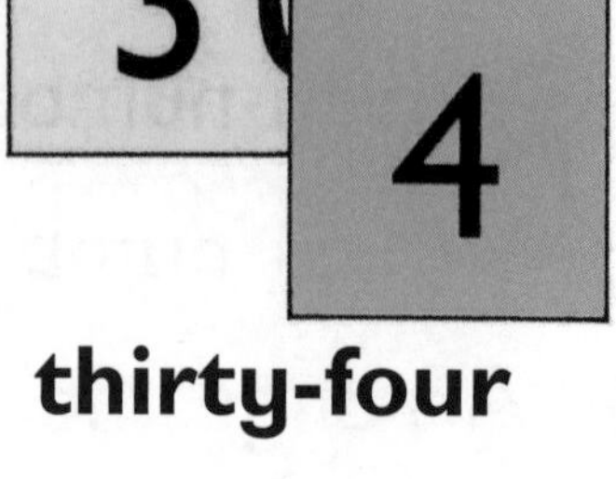
30
4

thirty-four

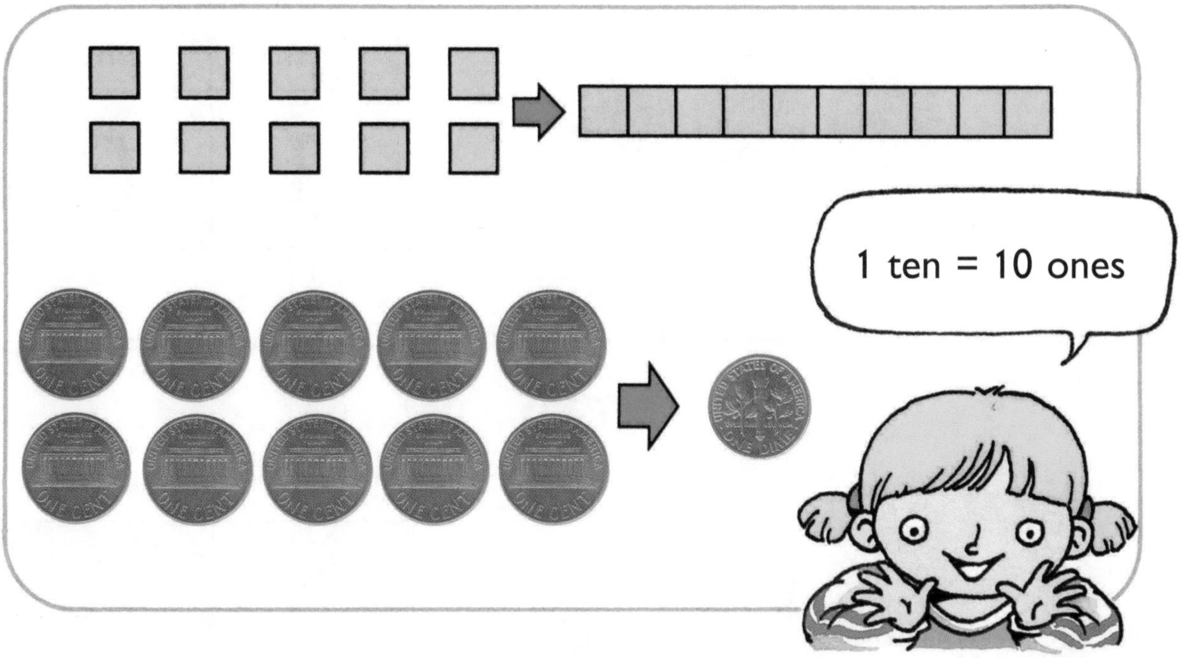

1. (a) 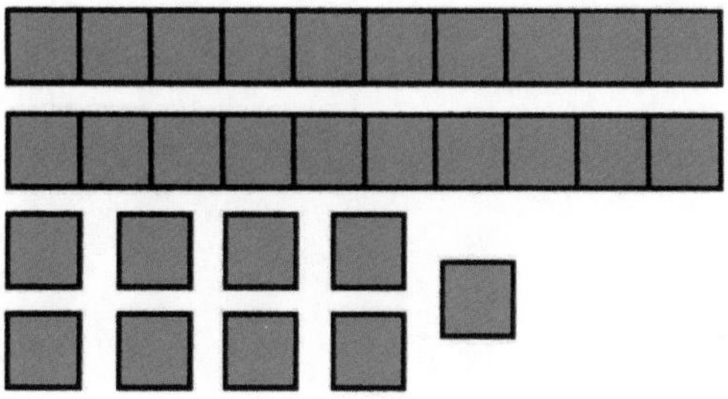

Tens	Ones
2	9

29 = ☐ tens ☐ ones

(b) 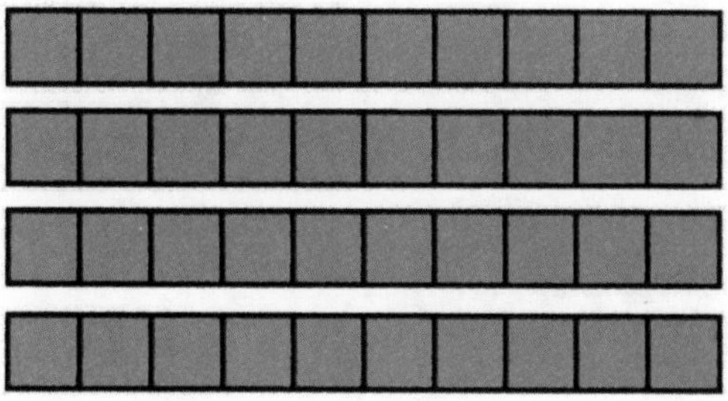

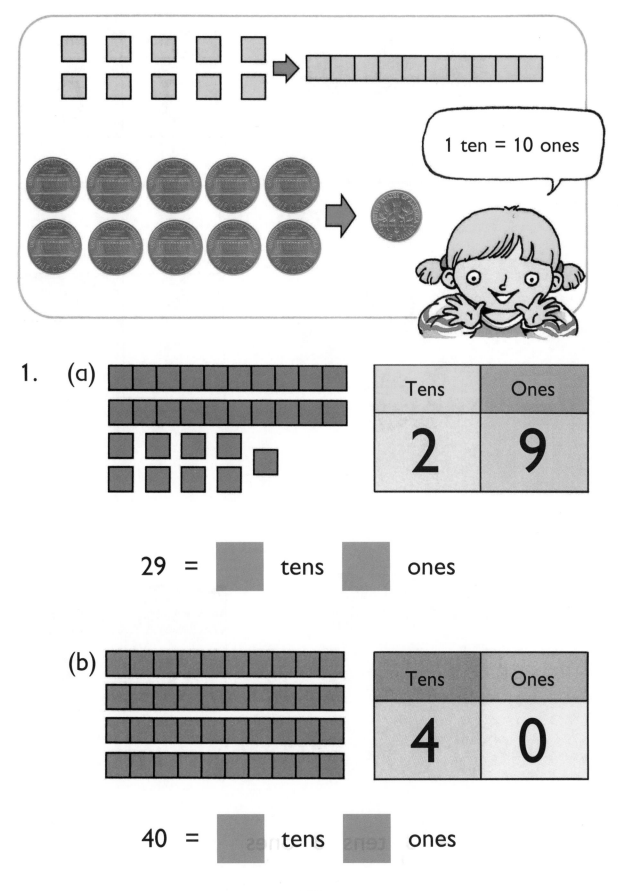

Tens	Ones
4	0

40 = ☐ tens ☐ ones

2. (a)

Tens	Ones
3	0

___ = 3 tens

(b)

Tens	Ones
2	3

___ = 2 tens 3 ones

(c)

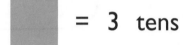

Tens	Ones
3	8

___ = 3 tens 8 ones

3. (a)

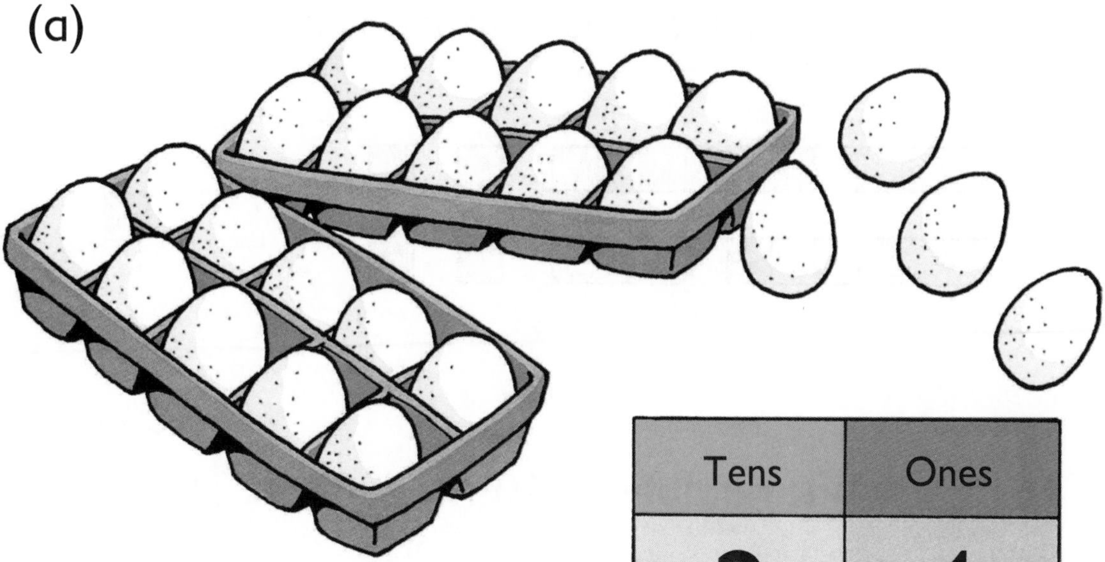

Tens	Ones
2	4

There are ☐ eggs.

(b)

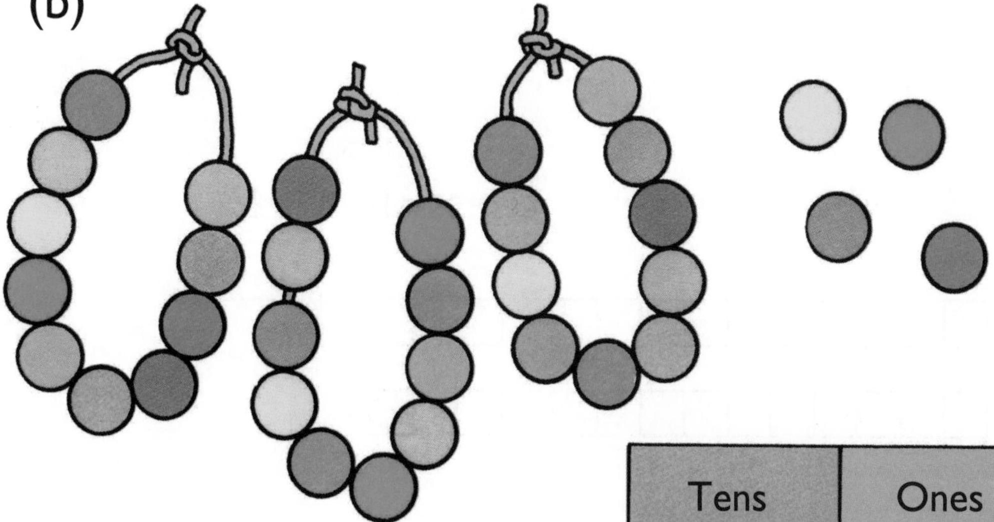

Tens	Ones
3	4

There are ☐ beads.

(c) Are there more eggs or more beads?
How many more?

Workbook Exercise 16

4. (a) What number is 1 more than 24?

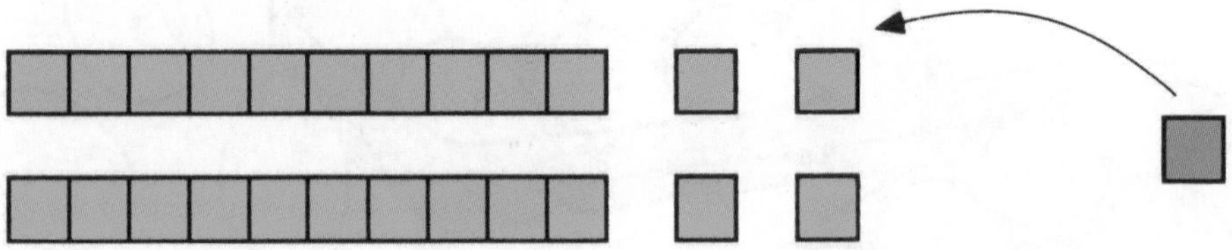

(b) What number is 10 more than 24?

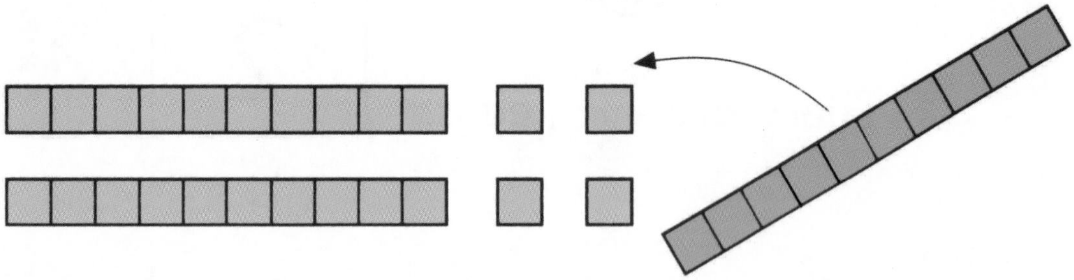

(c) What number is 1 less than 24?

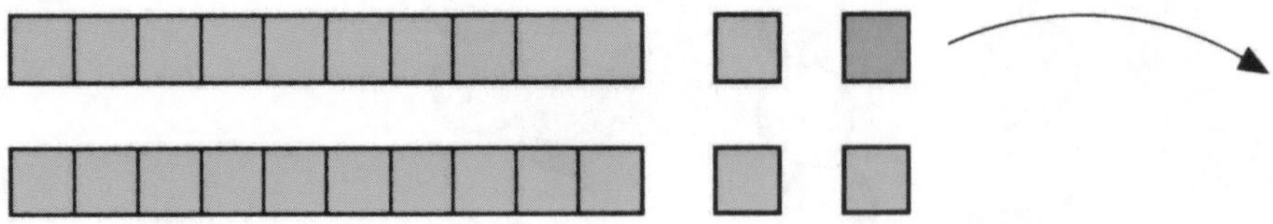

(d) What number is 10 less than 24?

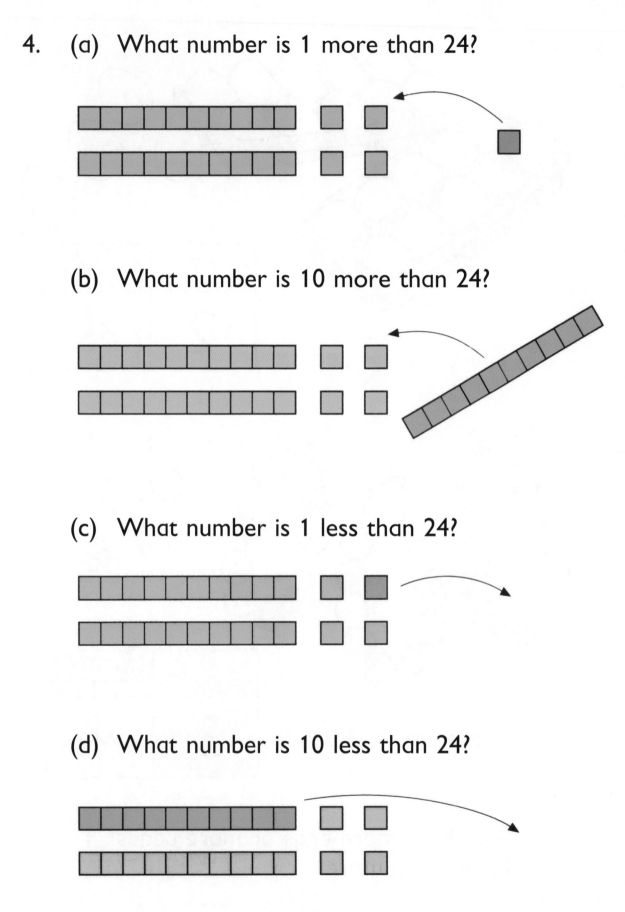

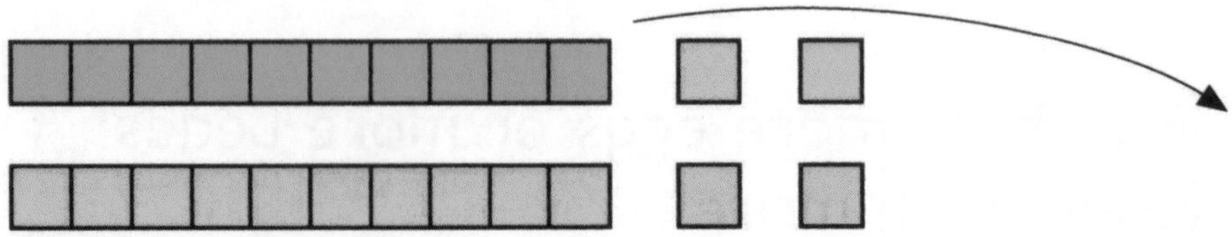

5. (a) What number is 1 more than 29?

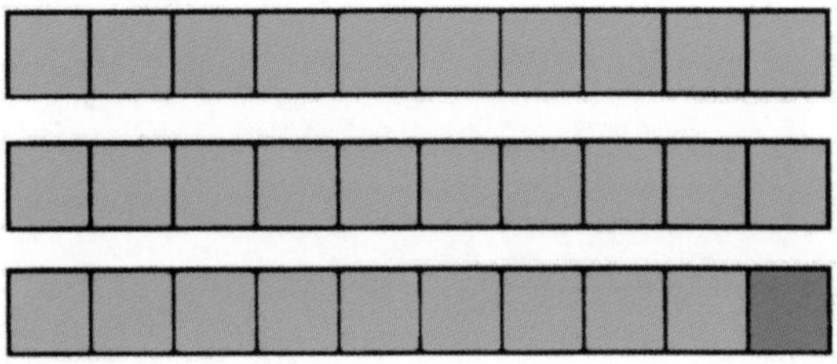

(b) What number is 1 less than 40?

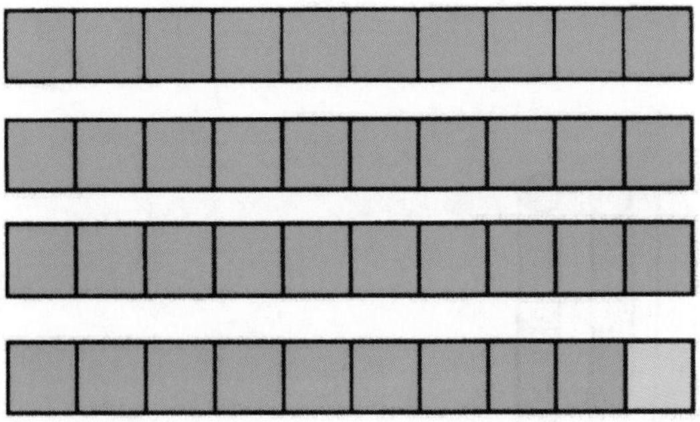

(c) What number is 10 more than 30?

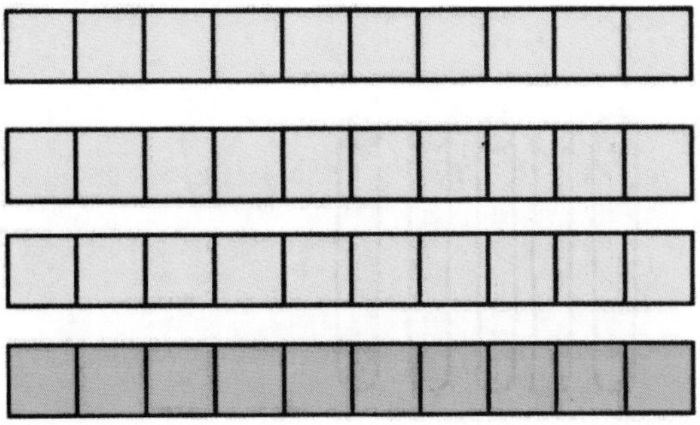

(d) What number is 10 less than 30?

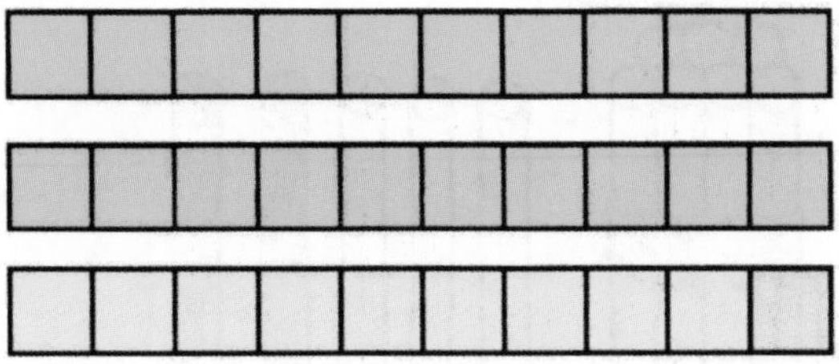

Workbook Exercise 17

3 Addition and Subtraction

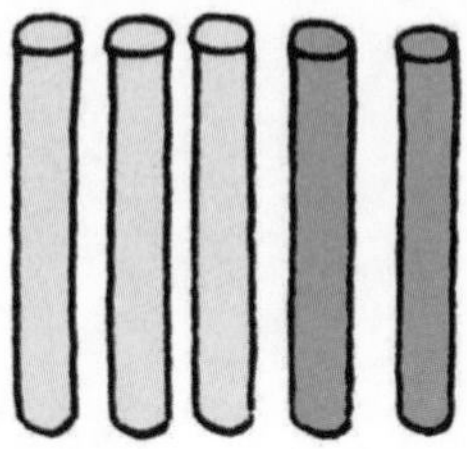

3 + 2 = ▢

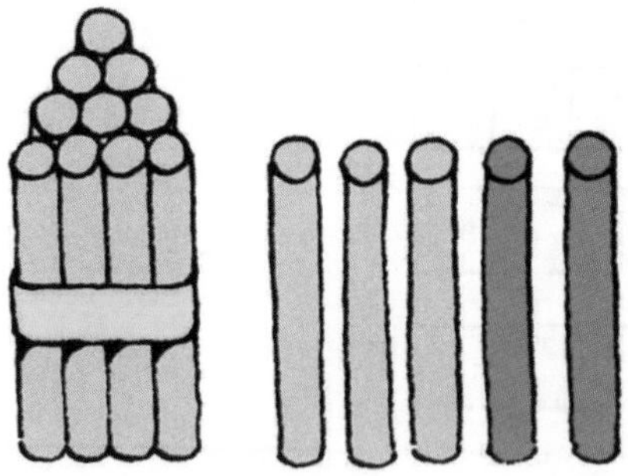

13 + 2 = ▢

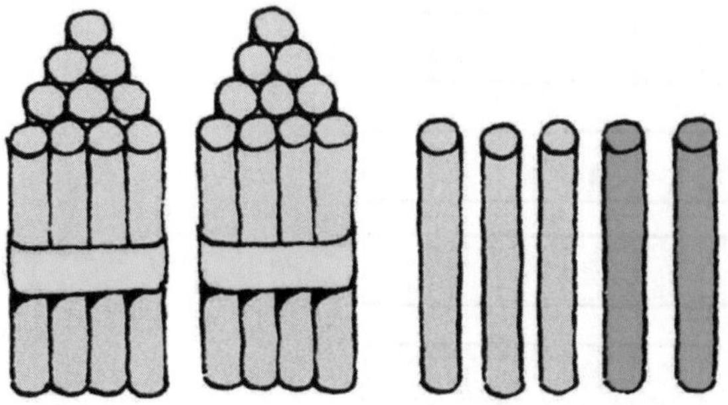

23 + 2 = ▢

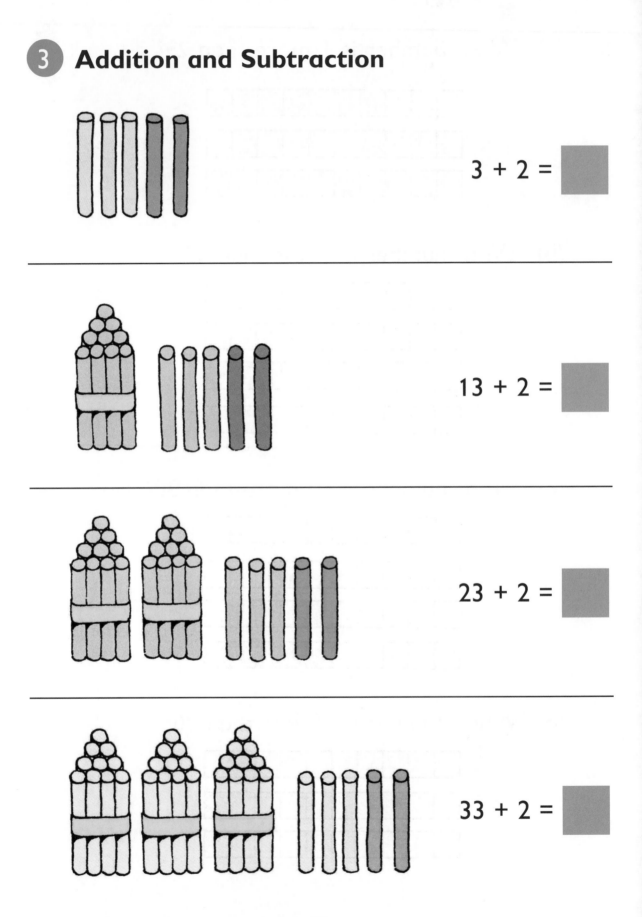

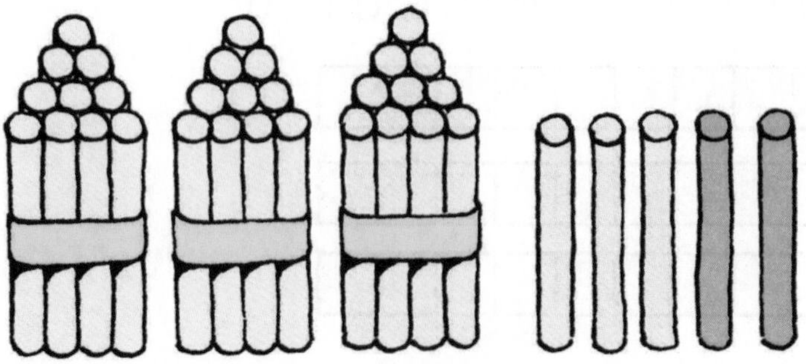

33 + 2 = ▢

$5 - 3 = \square$

$15 - 3 = \square$

$25 - 3 = \square$

$35 - 3 = \square$

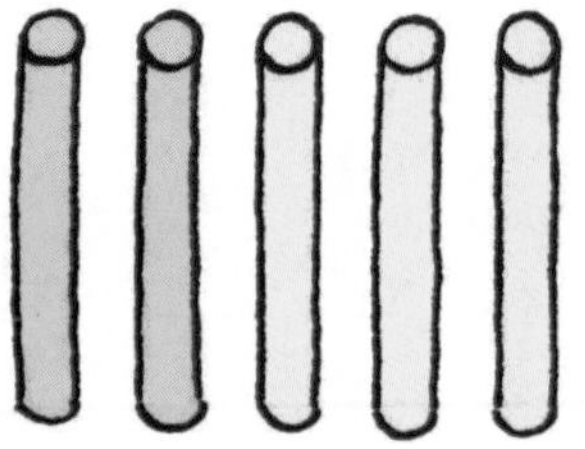

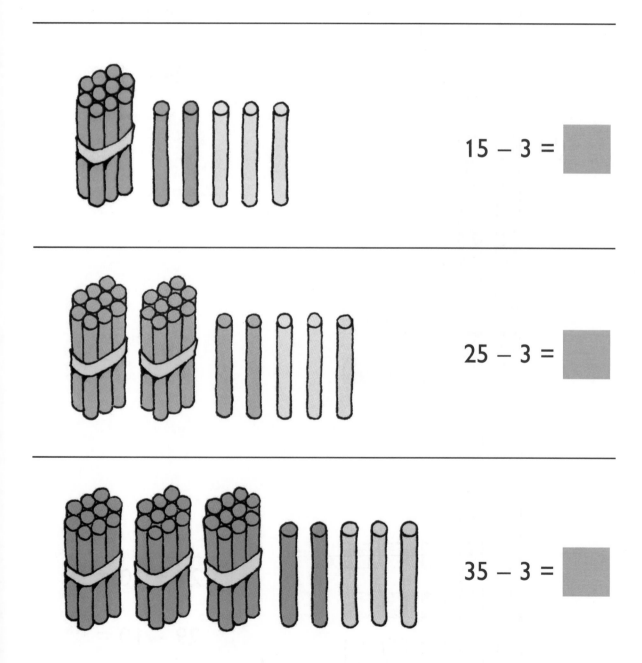

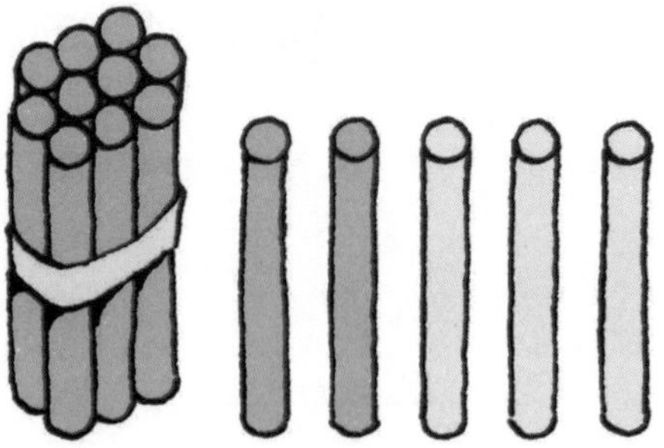

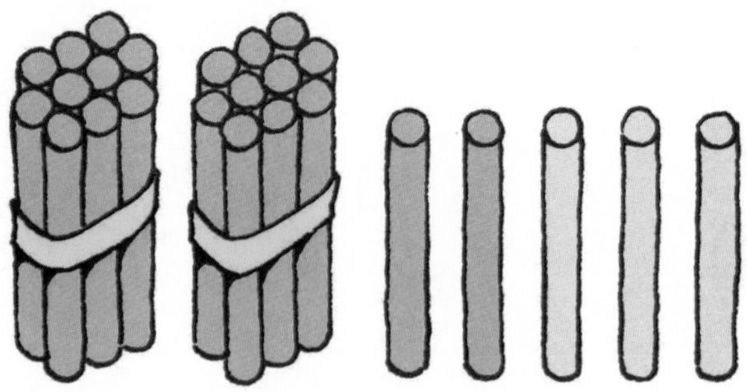

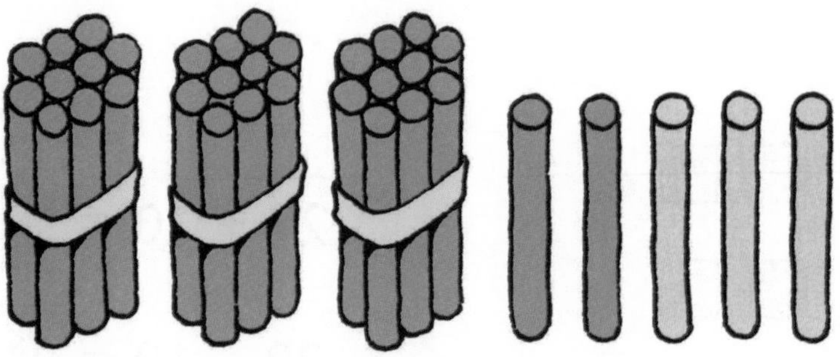

1. Add or subtract.

(a)

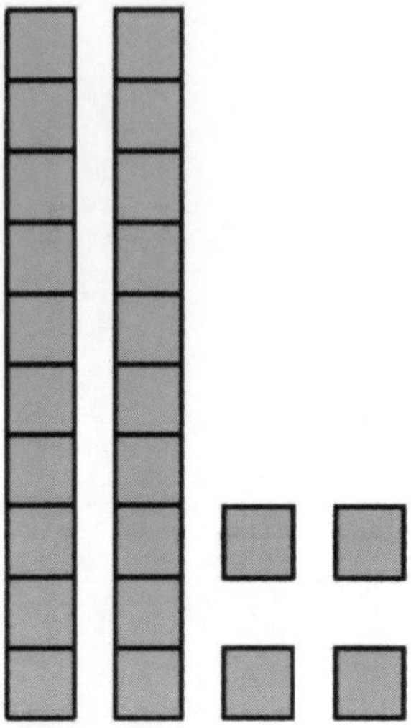

$24 + 4 =$ ☐

$24 - 4 =$ ☐

(b)

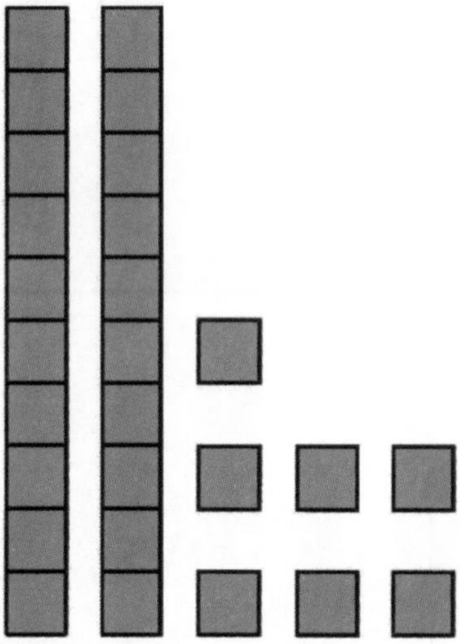

$27 + 3 =$ ☐

$27 - 3 =$ ☐

(c)

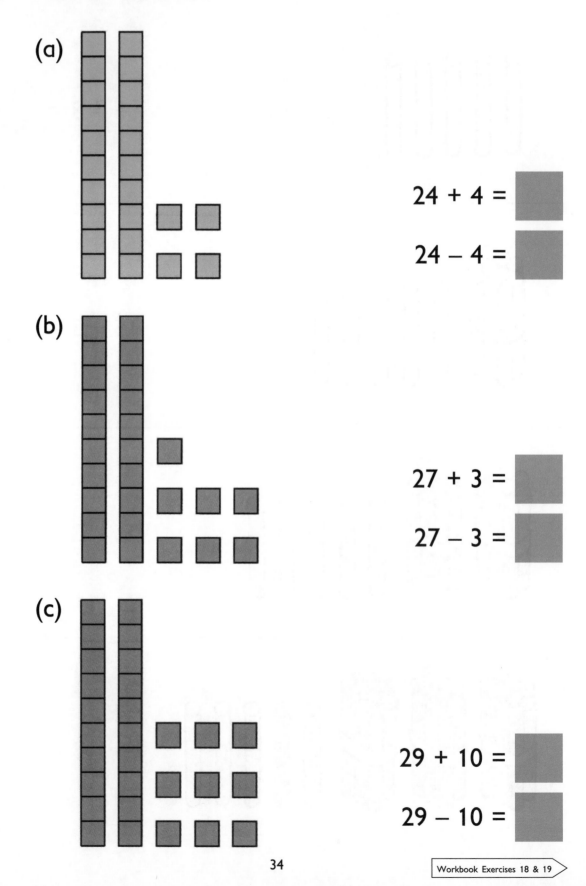

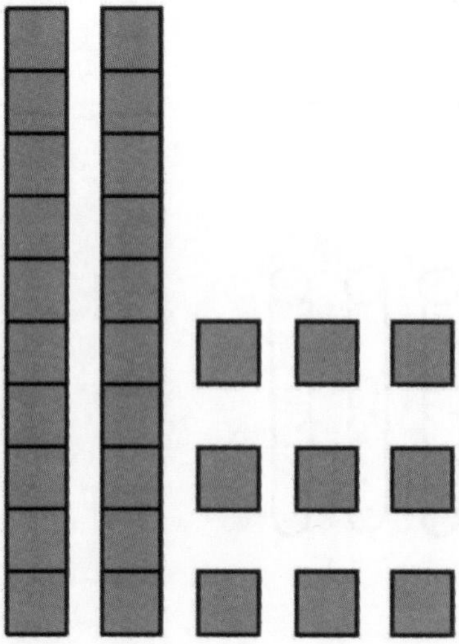

$29 + 10 =$ ☐

$29 - 10 =$ ☐

Workbook Exercises 18 & 19

2. Add 29 and 3.

29 + 3 = ☐

3. Subtract 2 from 31.

31 – 2 = ☐

Workbook Exercise 20

4. (a)

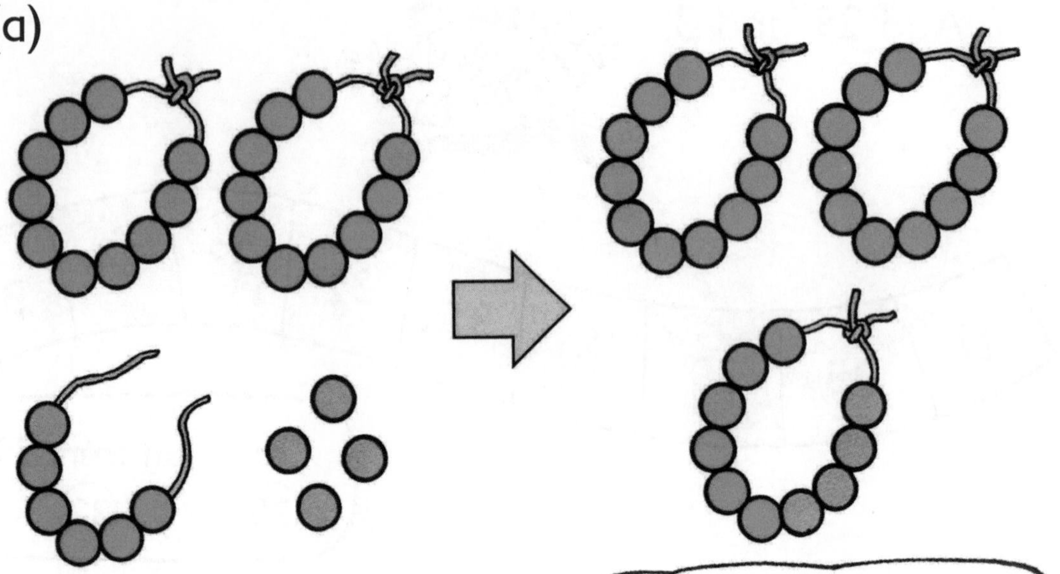

26 + 4 = ▢

(b)

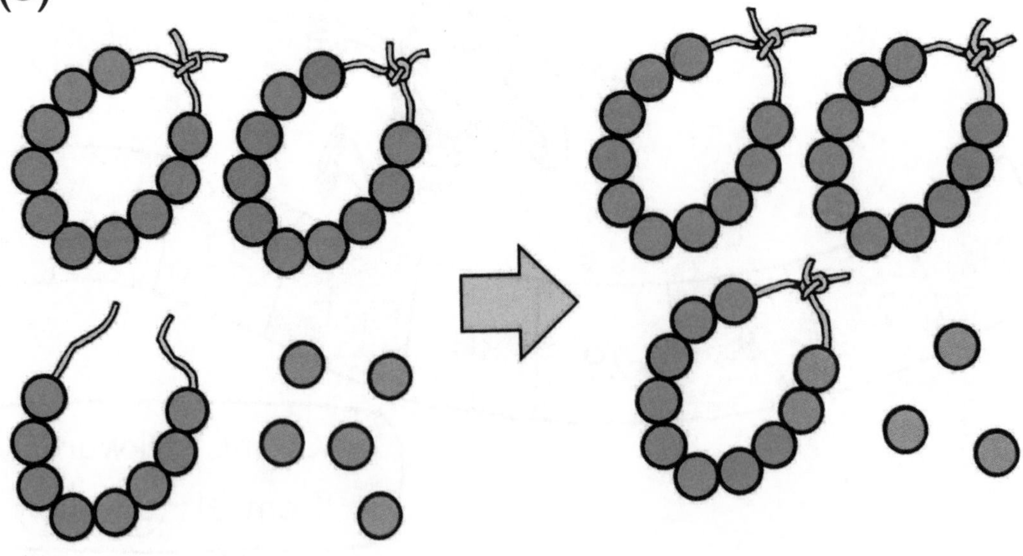

28 + 5 = ▢

5. (a)

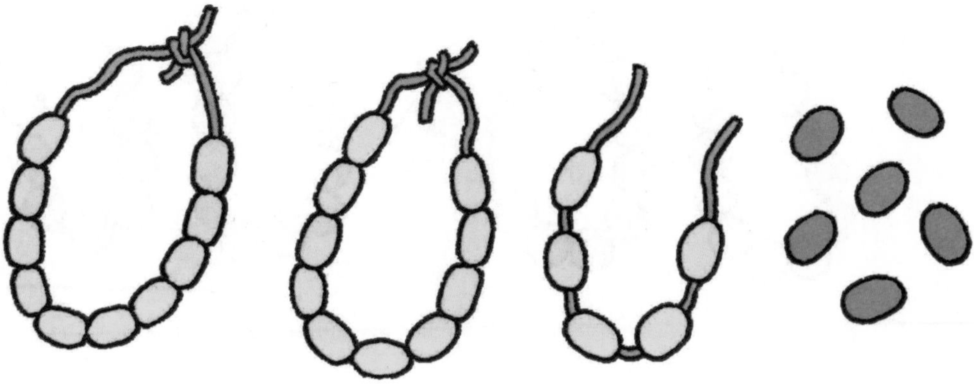

25 + 6 = ☐

(b)

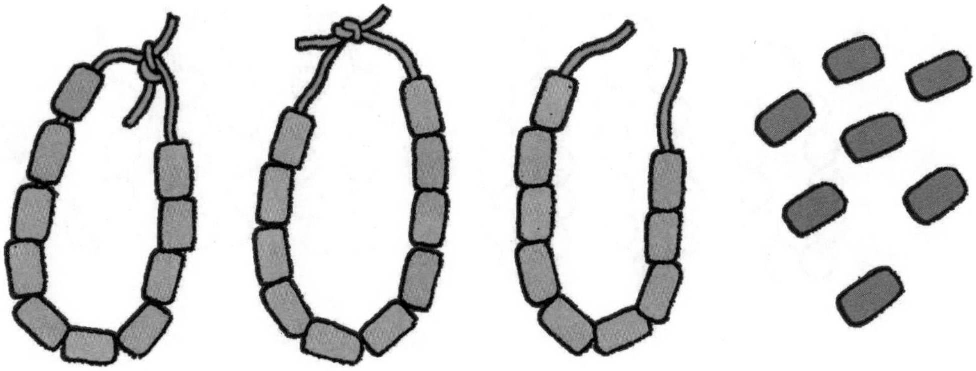

29 + 7 = ☐

(c)

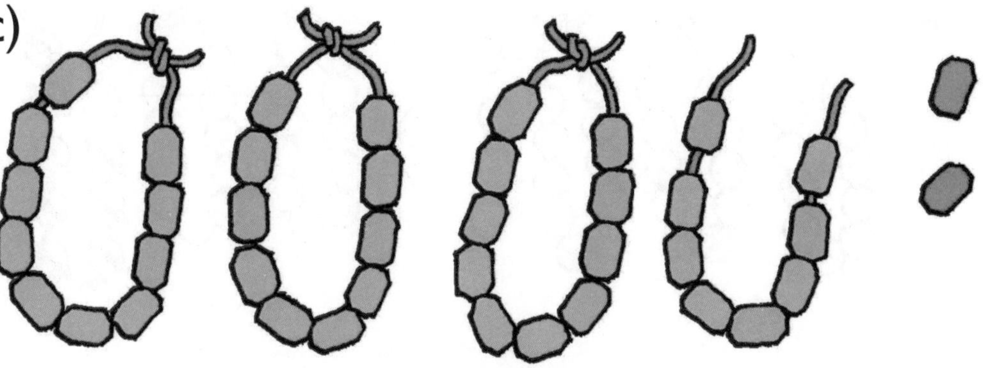

38 + 2 = ☐

Workbook Exercises 21 to 24

6. (a)

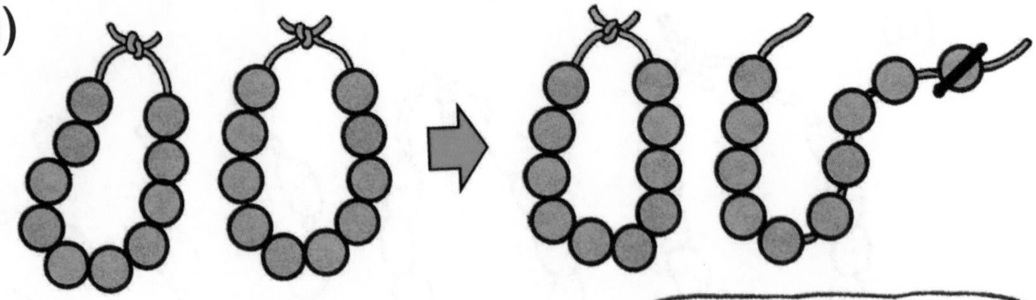

20 – 1 = ▢

(b)

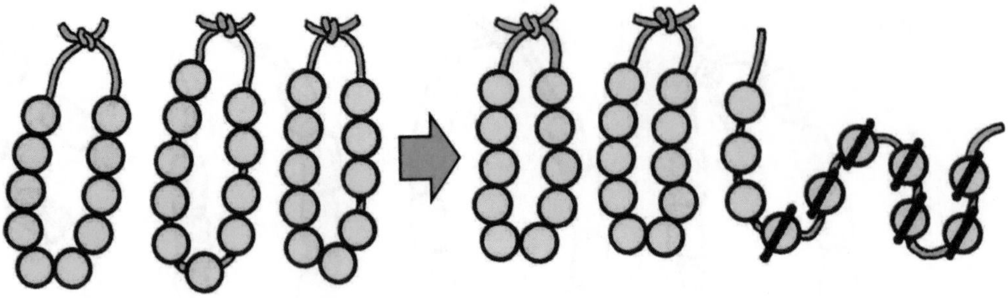

30 – 7 = ▢

(c)

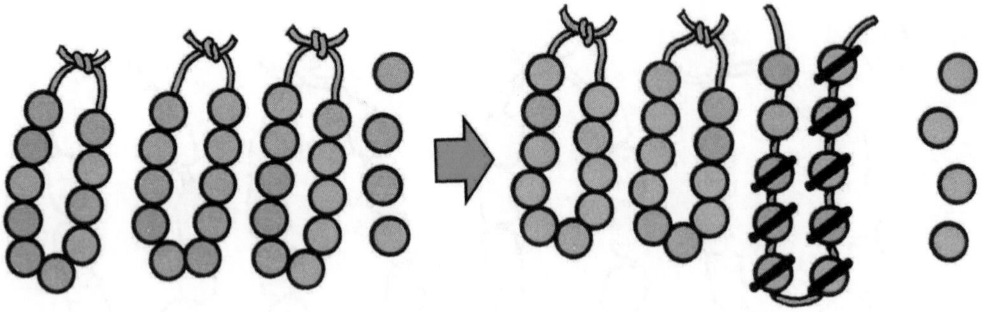

34 – 8 = ▢

7. (a)

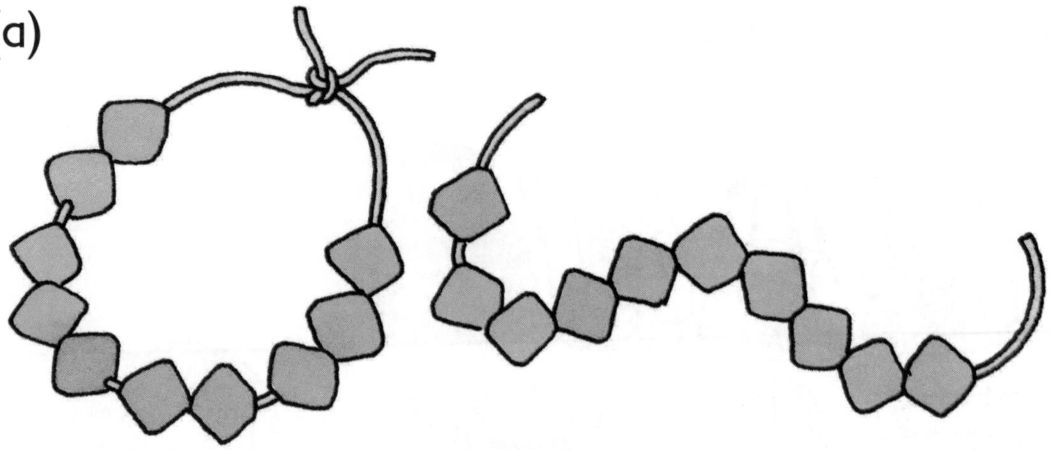

20 − 6 = ▢

(b)

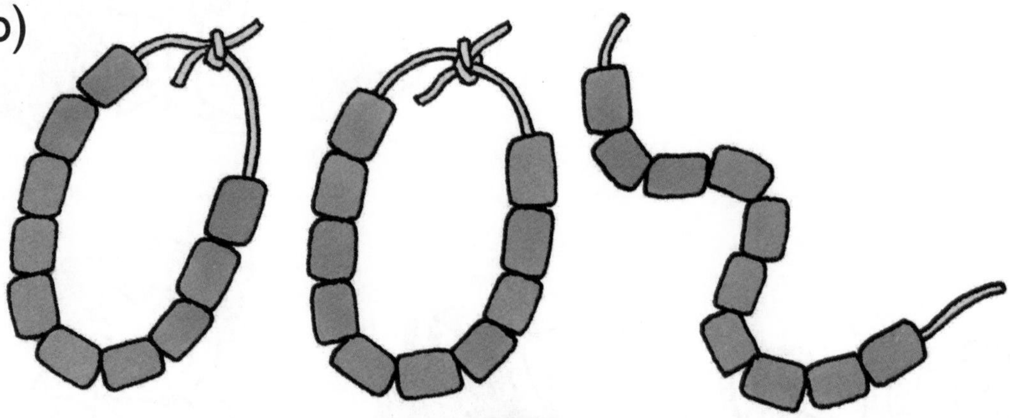

30 − 8 = ▢

(c)

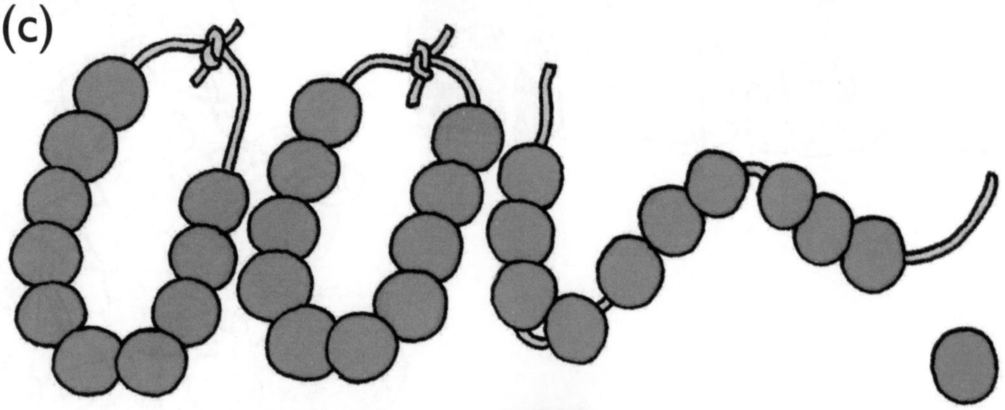

31 − 9 = ▢

Workbook Exercises 25 to 27

4 Adding Three Numbers

8 + 2 =

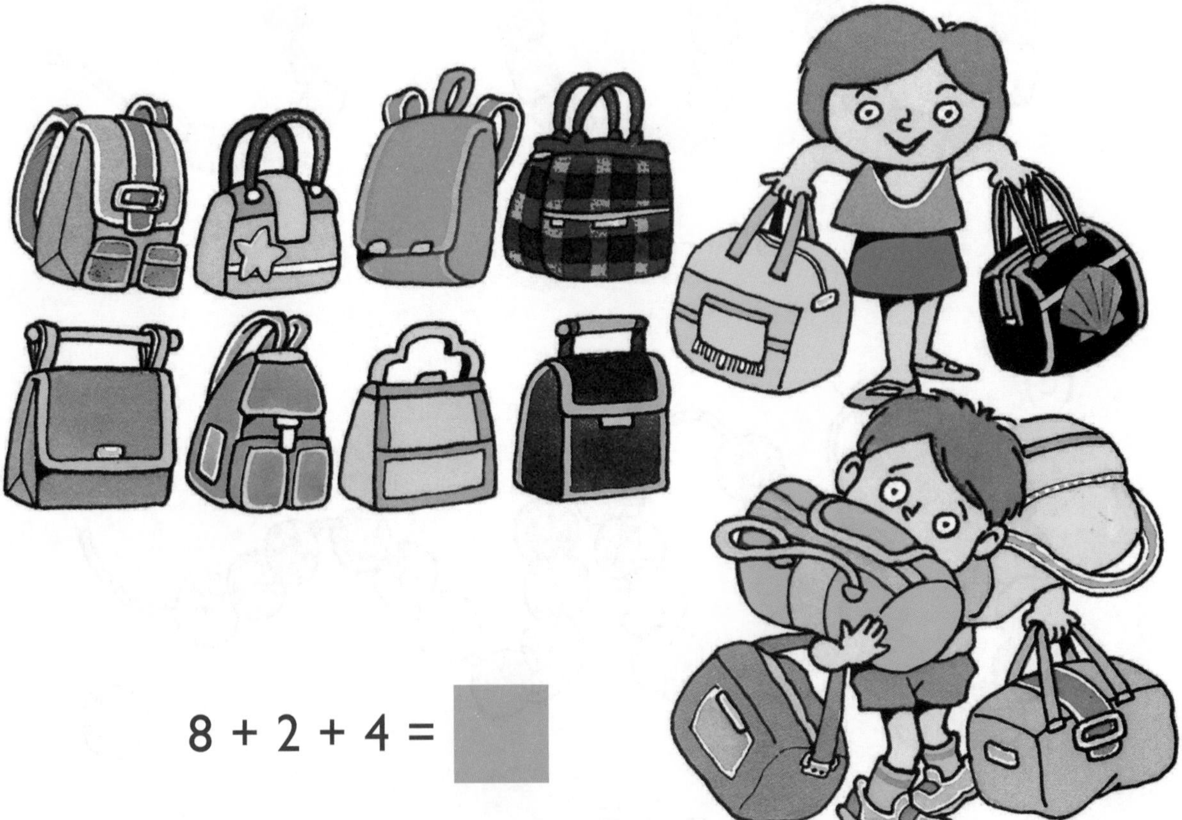

8 + 2 + 4 =

1. (a)

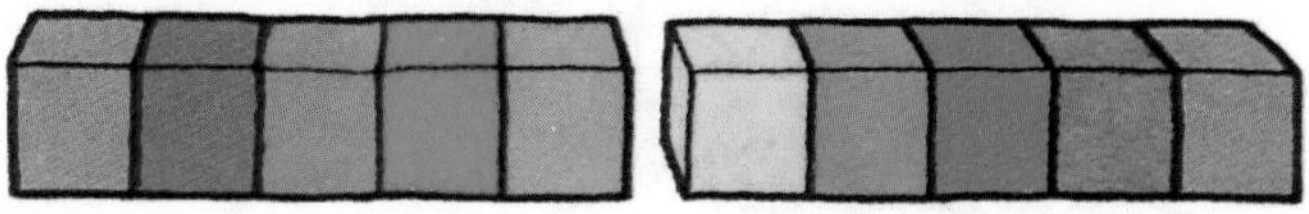

5 + 5 = ☐

(b)

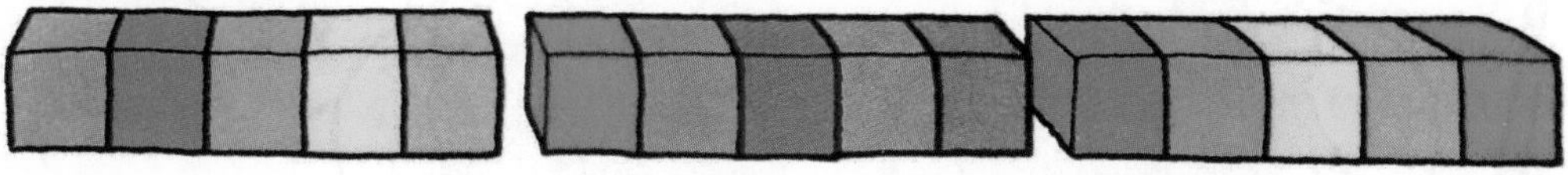

5 + 5 + 5 = ☐

2. Complete the addition sentences.

(a) 4 + 4 + 4 = ☐ (b) 6 + 4 + 3 = ☐

(c) 3 + 2 + 9 = ☐ (d) 6 + 6 + 6 = ☐

(e) 7 + 5 + 4 = ☐ (f) 8 + 6 + 2 = ☐

(g) 8 + 7 + 3 = ☐ (h) 8 + 8 + 8 = ☐

Workbook Exercises 28 & 29

4 Multiplication

1 Adding Equal Groups

Count each type of fruit.

5 + 5 + 5 = ☐

3 fives = ☐

There are 5 pears in each group.

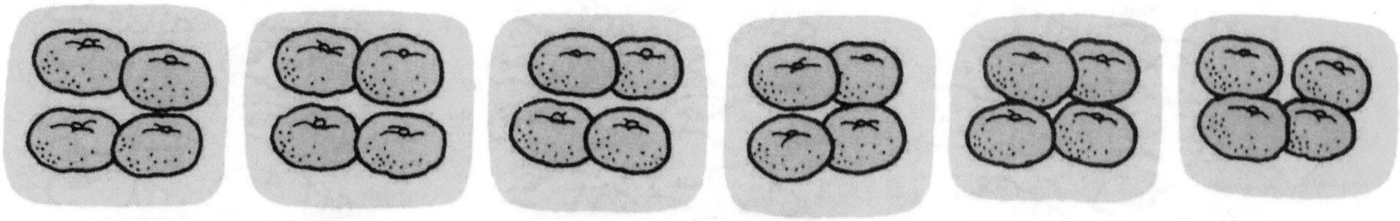

4 + 4 + 4 + 4 + 4 + 4 = ☐

6 fours = ☐

There are 4 oranges in each group.

6 + 6 = ☐

2 sixes = ☐

There are 6 pineapples in each group.

1. 

There are ☐ rabbits in each group.

There are ☐ rabbits altogether.

2. 

There are ☐ shells in each group.

There are ☐ shells altogether.

3. 

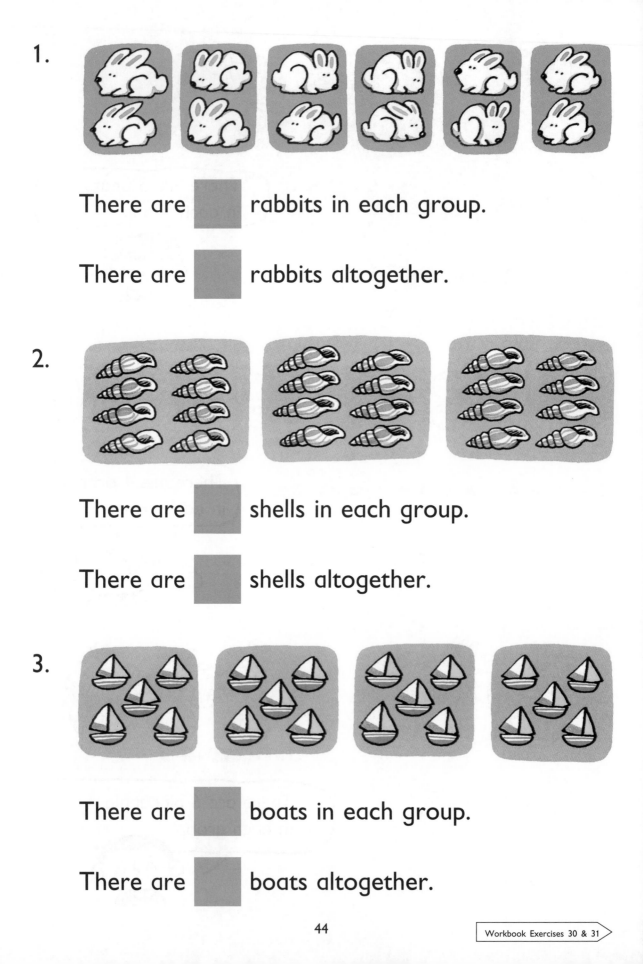

There are ☐ boats in each group.

There are ☐ boats altogether.

Workbook Exercises 30 & 31

4.

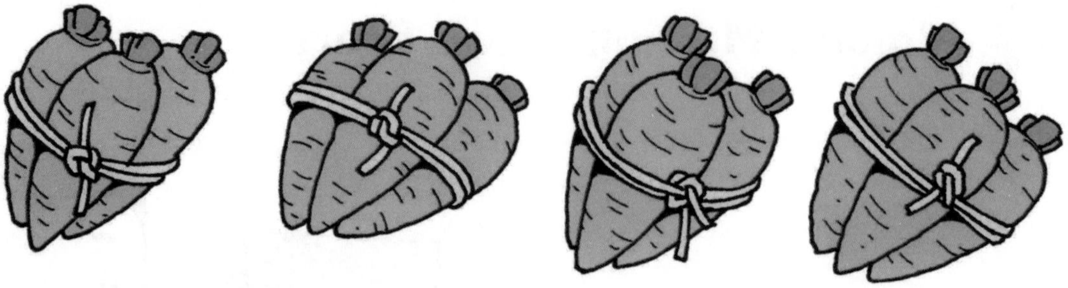

There are ☐ groups of 3.

There are ☐ carrots altogether.

5.

There are ☐ groups of 4.

There are ☐ cakes altogether.

6.

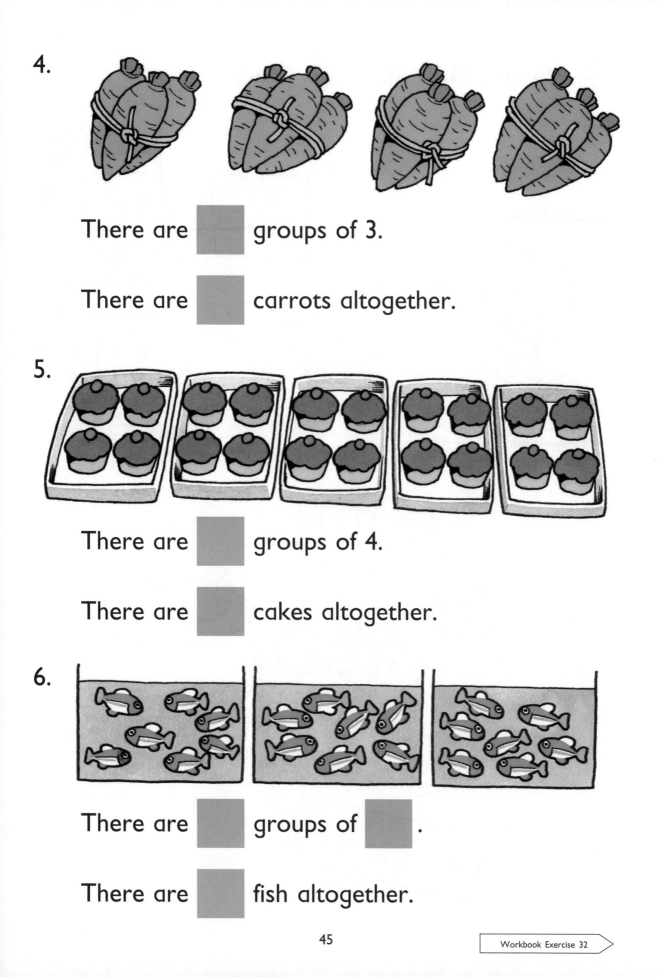

There are ☐ groups of ☐ .

There are ☐ fish altogether.

2 Making Multiplication Stories

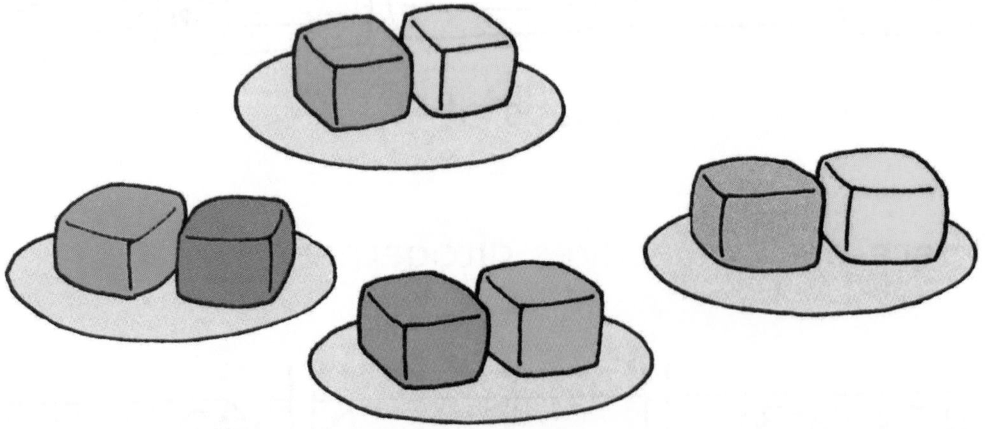

4 twos

4 groups of 2

This is **multiplication**.
It means **putting together equal groups**.

We write the number sentence:

$$\mathbf{4 \times 2 = 8}$$

Multiply 4 and 2.
The answer is 8.

There are 4 equal groups.
There are 2 blocks in each group.
There are 8 blocks altogether.

1. Make up a story for each number sentence.

(a)

$4 \times 3 = 12$

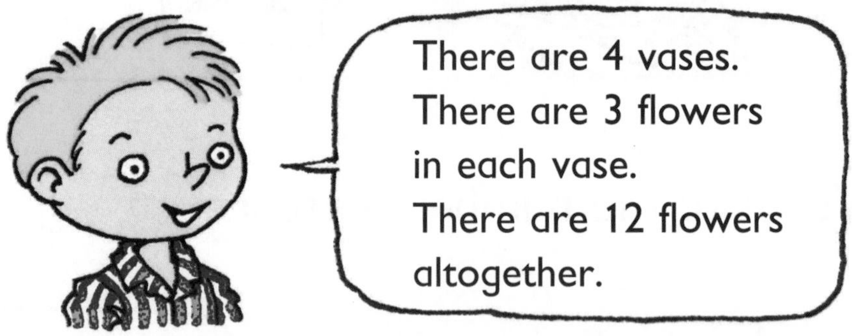

There are 4 vases.
There are 3 flowers in each vase.
There are 12 flowers altogether.

(b)

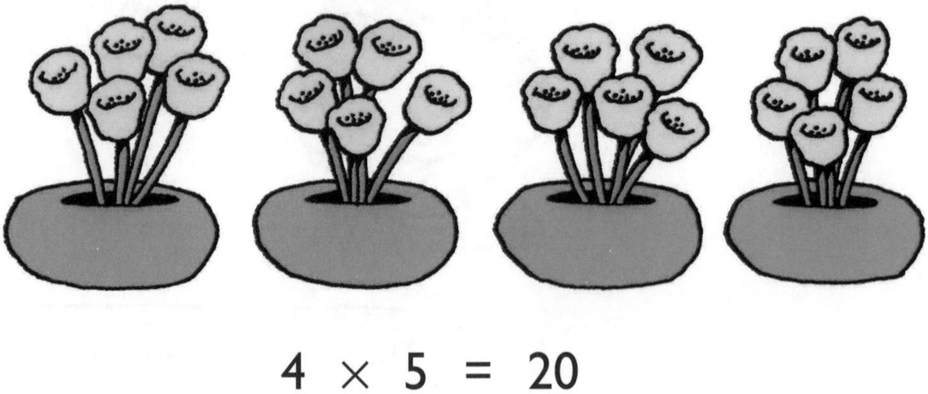

$4 \times 5 = 20$

(c)

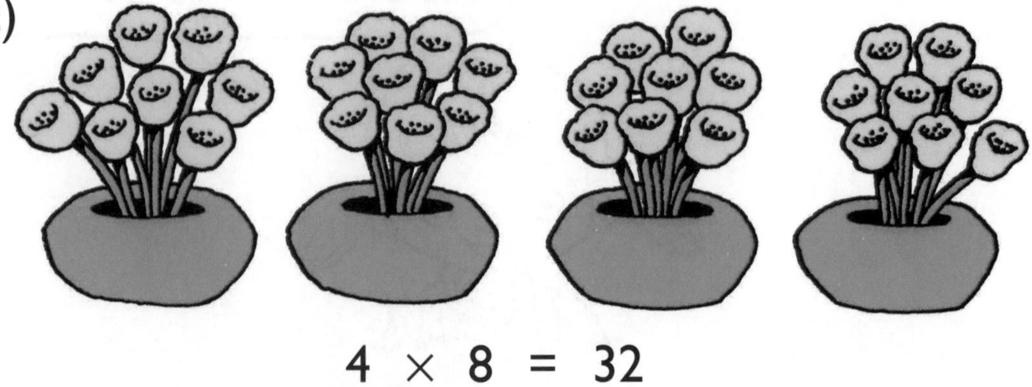

$4 \times 8 = 32$

2. Make up a story for each number sentence.

(a)

$4 \times 6 = 24$

(b)

$6 \times 4 = 24$

Workbook Exercises 33 & 34

3 Multiplication Within 40

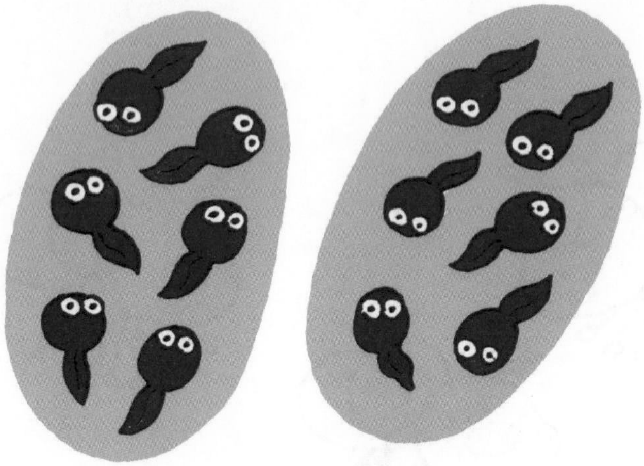

$2 \times 6 = \square$

$4 \times 5 = \square$

1.

How many pears are there altogether?

$$3 \times 2 = \square$$

There are ___ pears altogether.

2.

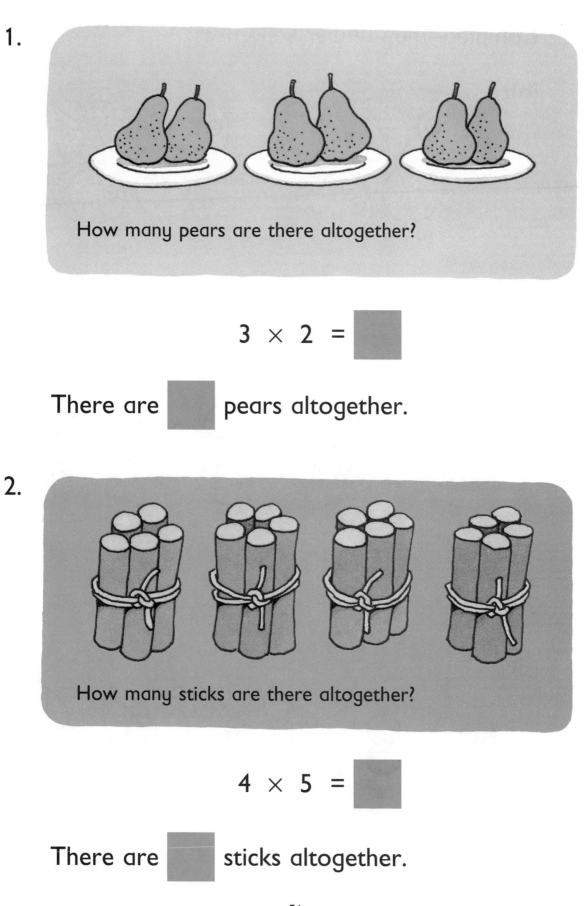

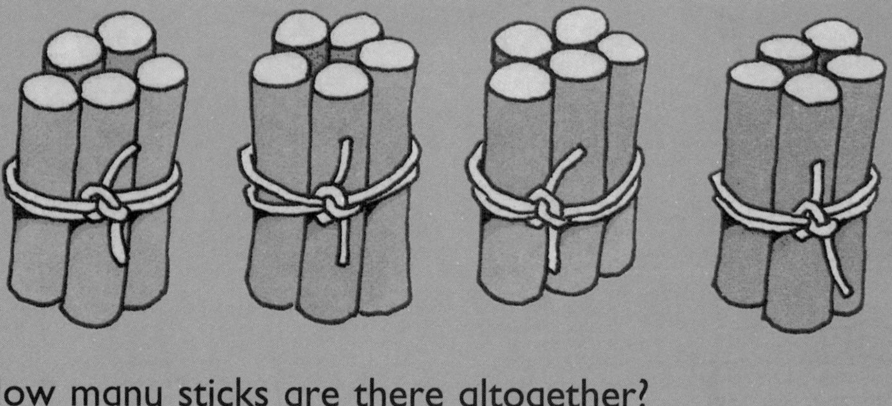

How many sticks are there altogether?

$$4 \times 5 = \square$$

There are ___ sticks altogether.

3. Complete the number sentences.

(a)

2 × ☐ = ☐

(b)

☐ × ☐ = ☐

(c)

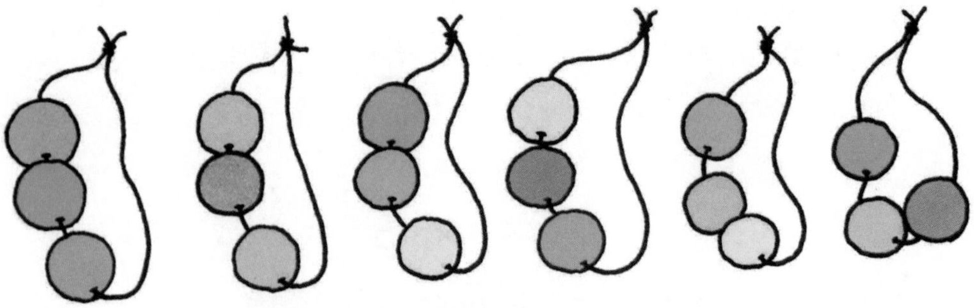

☐ × ☐ = ☐

Workbook Exercise 35

4.

There are 6 stamps in each row.

How many stamps are there in 3 rows?

$3 \times 6 =$ ☐

There are ☐ stamps.

5.

Lily made these squares with straws.

How many straws did she use?

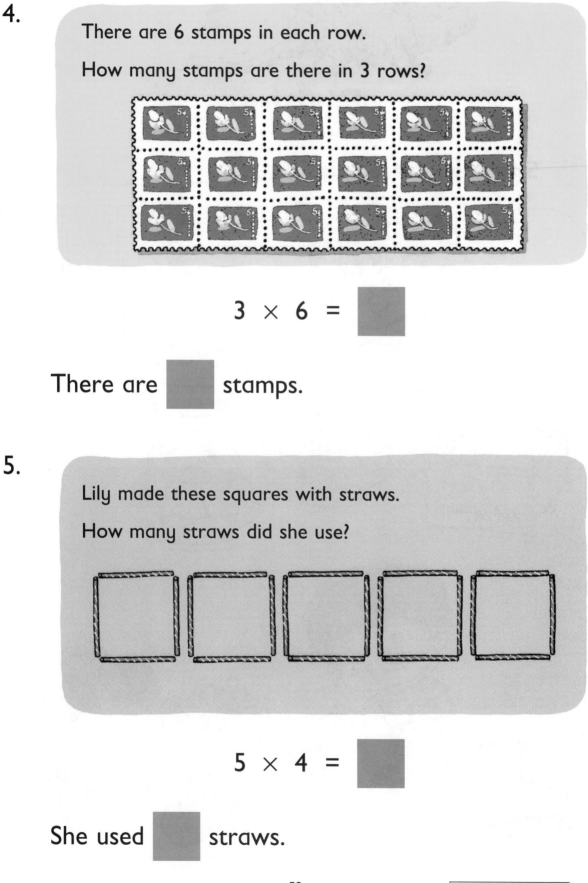

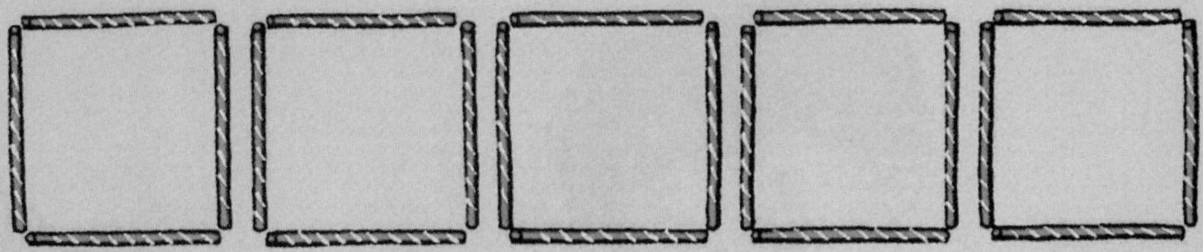

$5 \times 4 =$ ☐

She used ☐ straws.

Workbook Exercise 36

5

Division

1 Sharing and Grouping

I put 15 apples equally on 3 plates.

Divide 15 apples into 3 equal groups.

There are ____ apples in each group.

I put 3 apples in a group.

Divide 15 apples into groups of 3.

There are ___ groups.

1. Divide 10 children into 2 equal groups.
How many children are there in each group?

There are   children in each group.

2. Share 12 kiwis equally between 2 children.
How many kiwis does each child get?

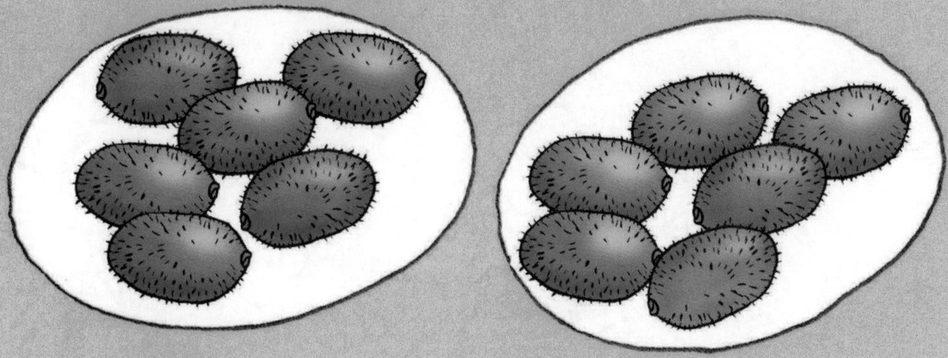

Each child gets   kiwis.

3. Put 14 crayons equally into 2 boxes.
How many crayons are there in each box?

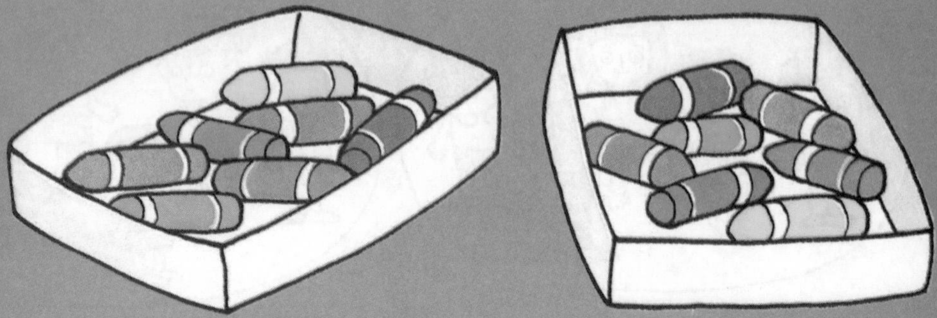

There are ▢ crayons in each box.

Workbook Exercises 37 & 38

4. There are 6 flowers.
Put 3 flowers in a vase.
How many vases are needed?

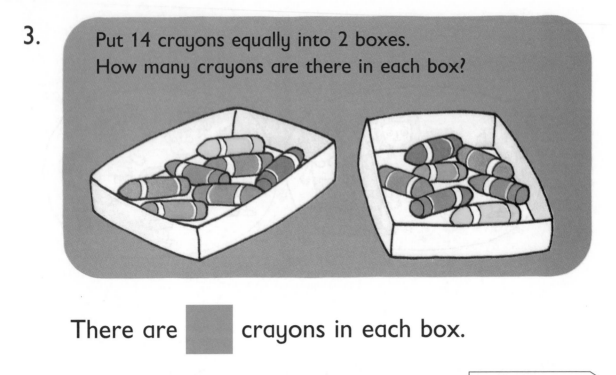

▢ vases are needed.

5.

There are 20 coins.
Put 5 coins in a set.
How many sets are there?

There are ☐ sets.

6.

Divide 12 mangoes into groups of 3.
How many groups are there?

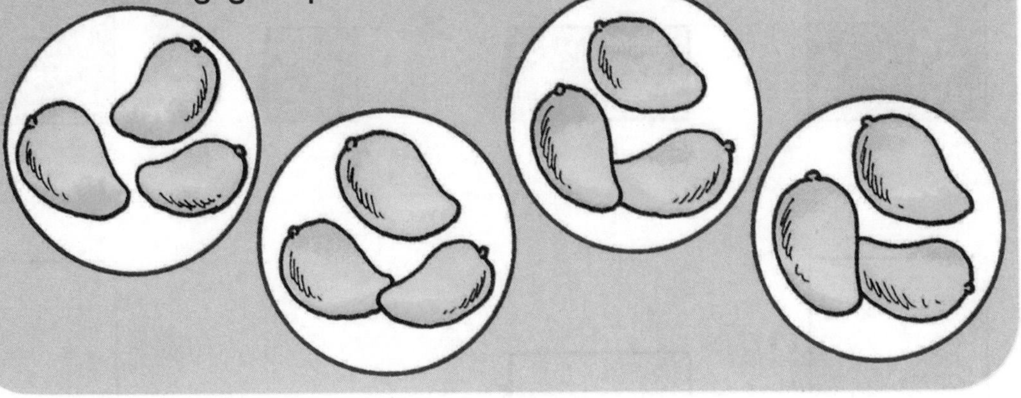

There are ☐ groups.

Workbook Exercises 39 & 40

Halves and Quarters

1 Making Halves and Quarters

Fold a piece of square paper into **halves**.

Then fold it into **quarters**.

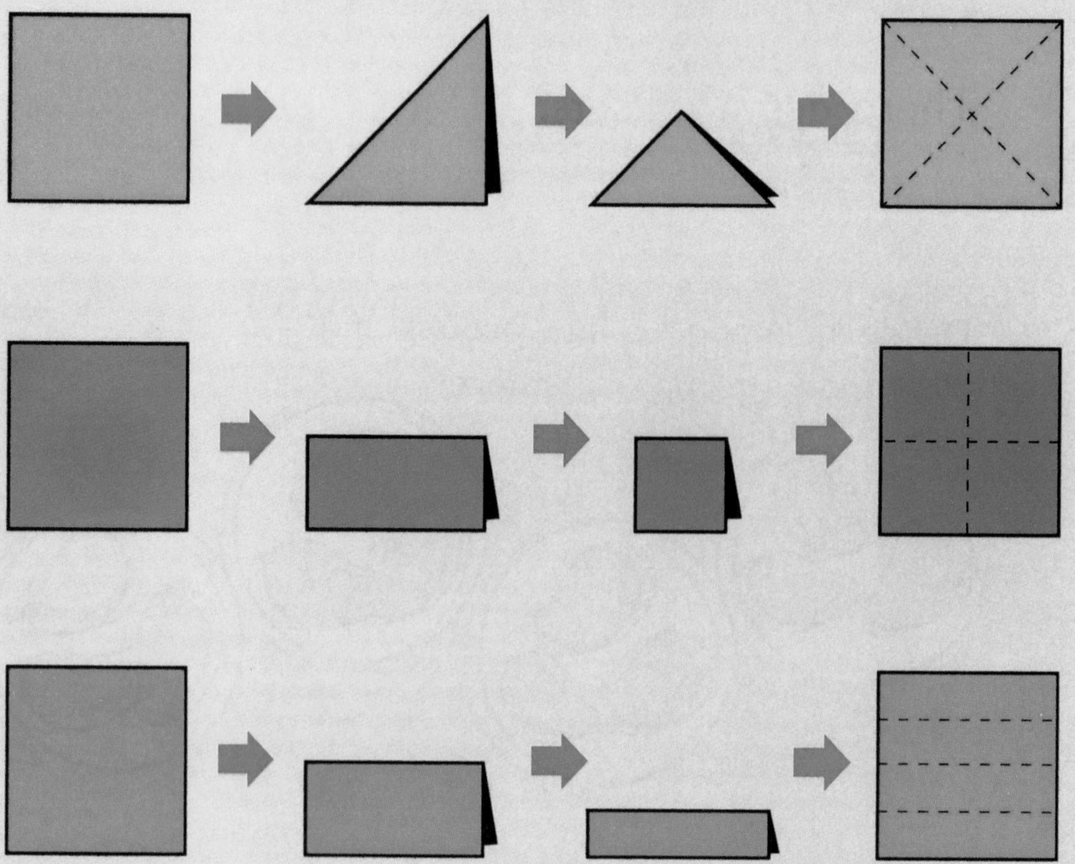

1.

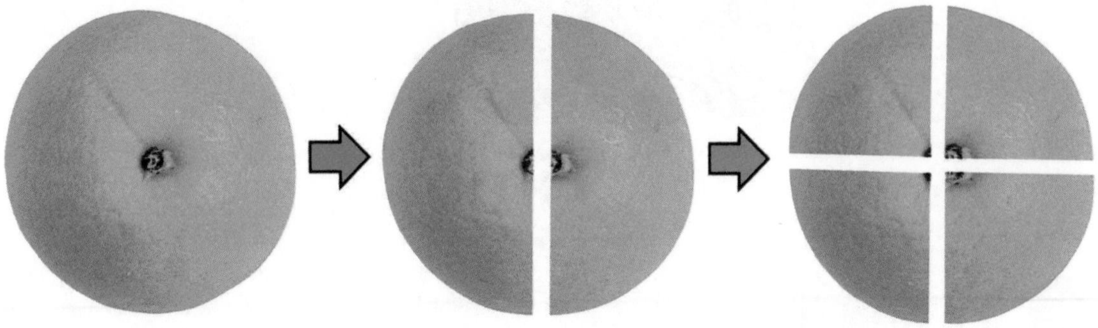

a whole  halves  quarters

2. Which pictures show halves?

(a)

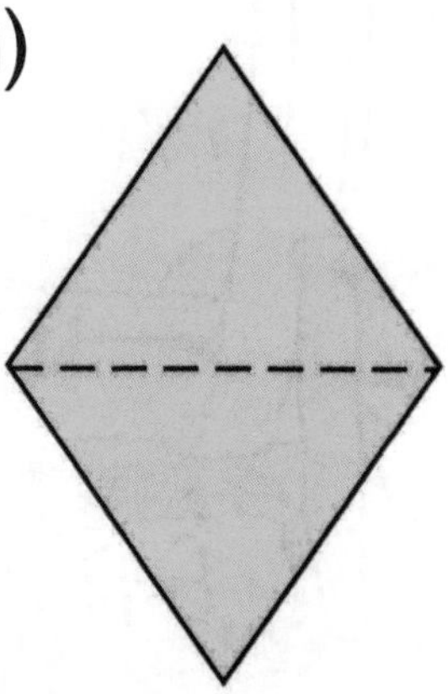

(b)

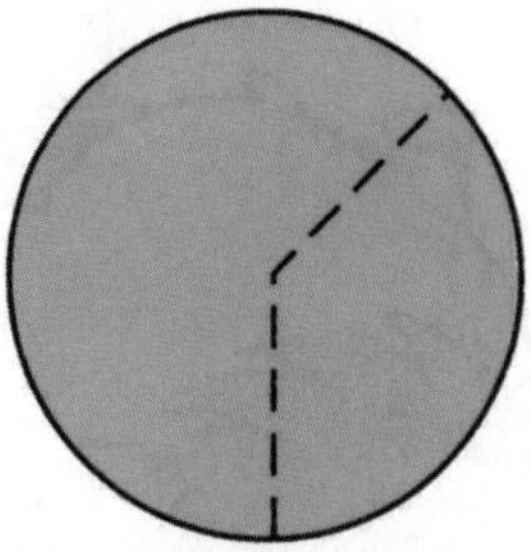

(c)

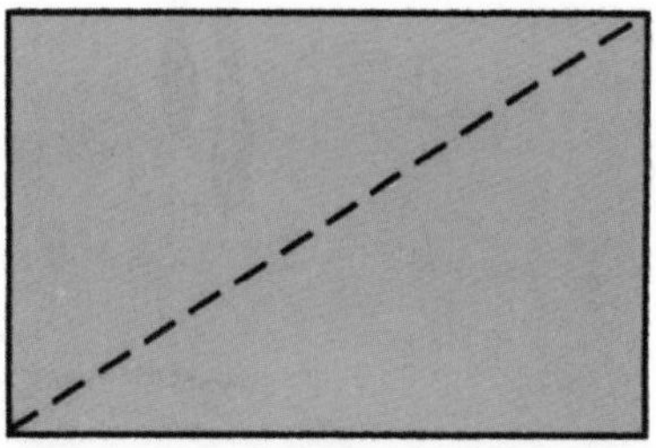

3. Which pictures show quarters?

(a)

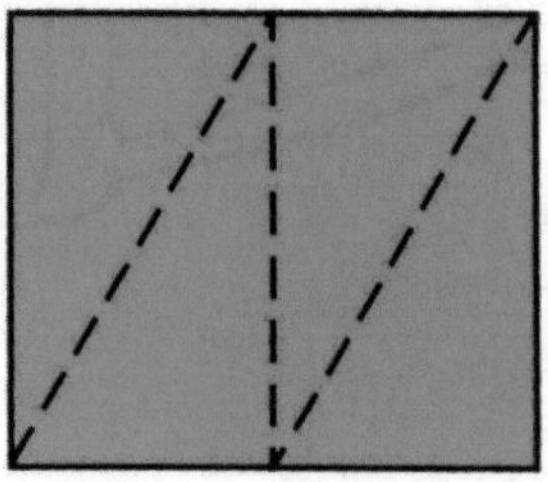

(b)

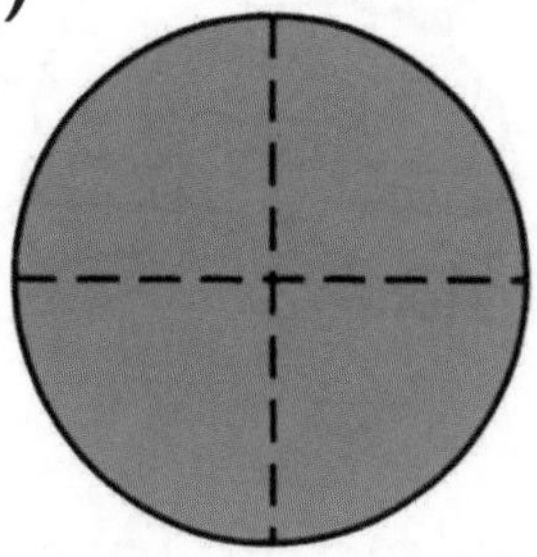

(c)

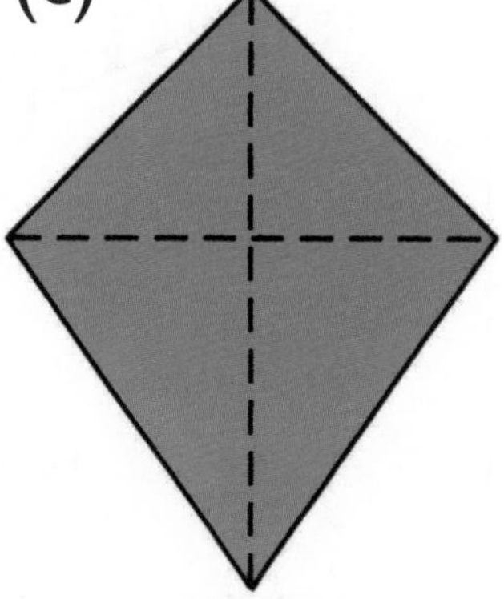

Workbook Exercises 41 to 43

7

Time

1 Telling Time

It is 6 o'clock in the morning.

1. What time is it?

Workbook Exercise 44

2.

It is 4 o'clock.

It is **half past** 4.

It is ____ o'clock.

It is half past ____ .

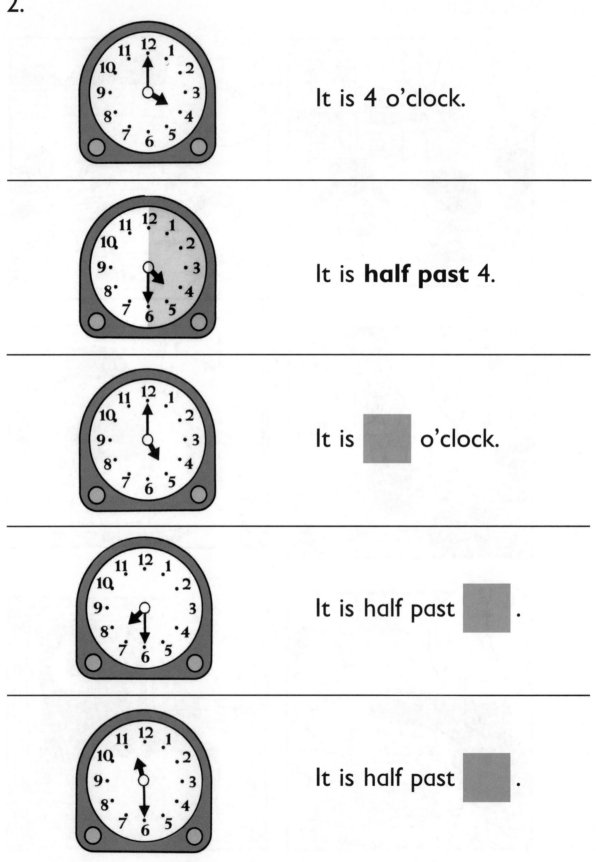

It is half past ____ .

3. What time is it?

Workbook Exercise 45

8

Numbers to 100

1 Tens and Ones

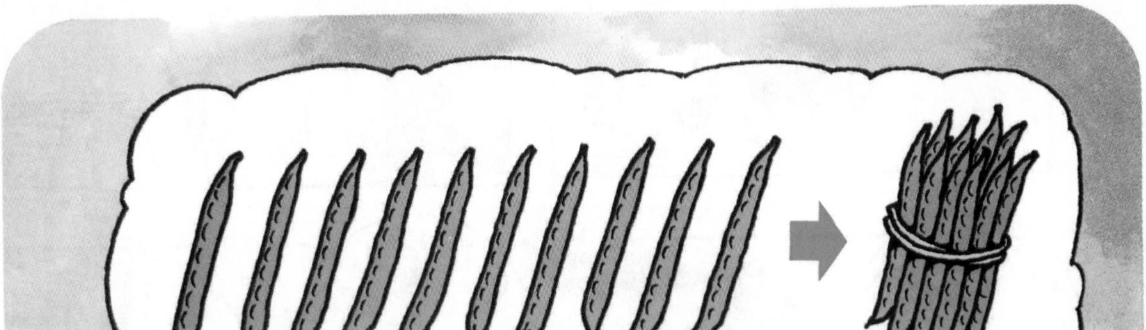

Count by tens.

50

fifty

5 tens = 50

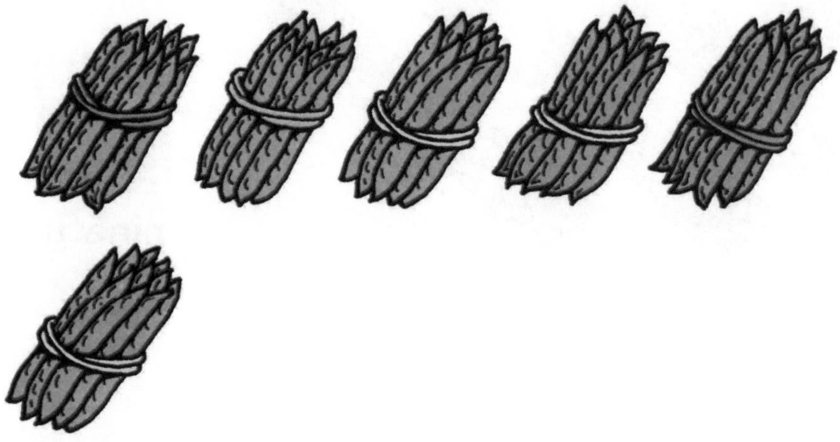

60

sixty

6 tens = 60

70

seventy

___ tens = 70

80

eighty

☐ tens = 80

90

ninety

☐ tens = 90

100

one hundred

☐ tens = 100

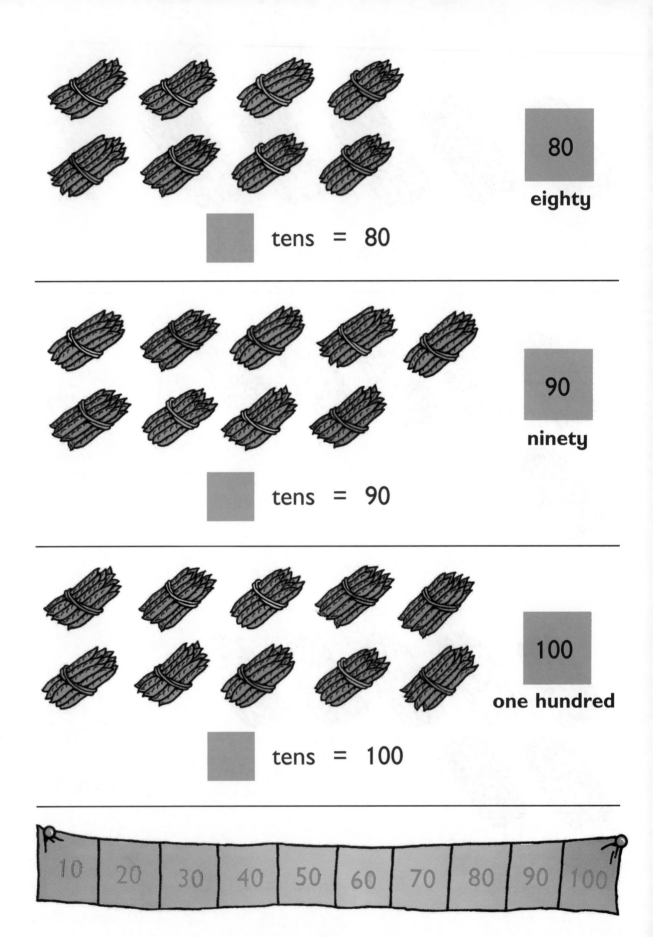

1. Count the tens.

(a)

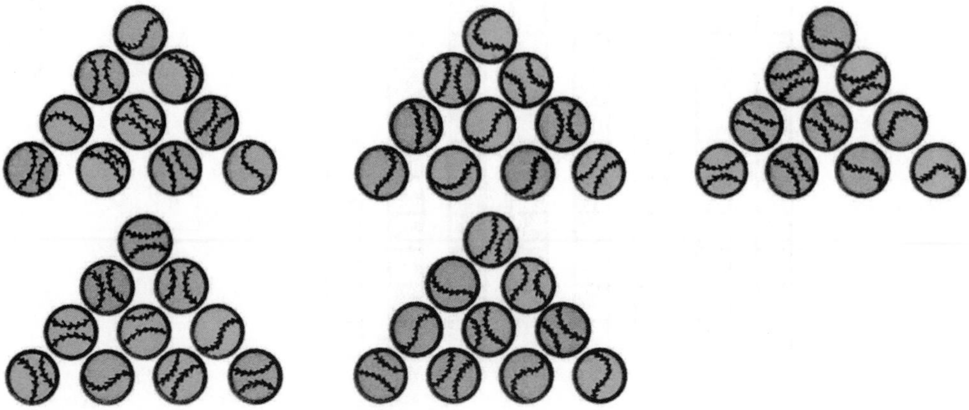

☐ tens = ☐

(b)

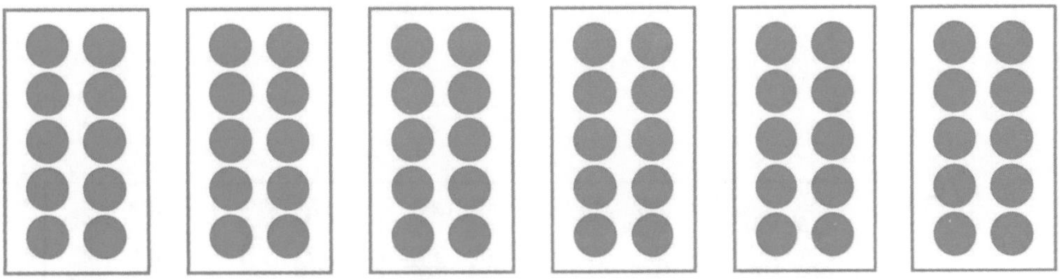

☐ tens = ☐

(c)

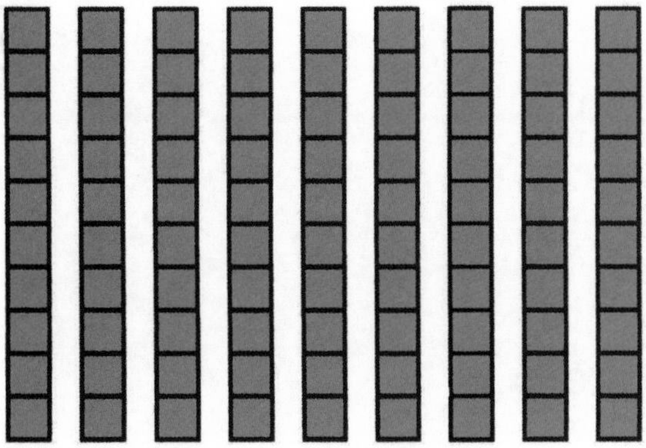

☐ tens = ☐

Workbook Exercise 46

2. (a)

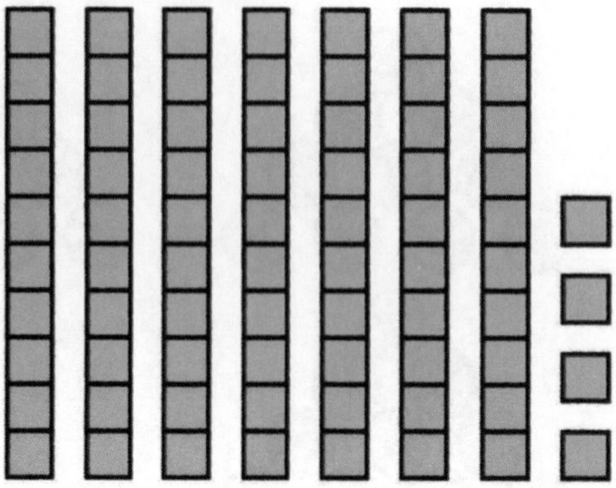

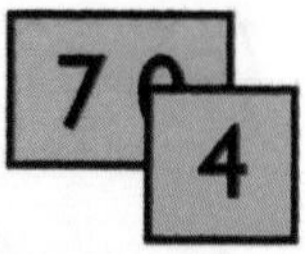

seventy-four

74 is 70 and 4.

74 = ☐ tens ☐ ones

(b)

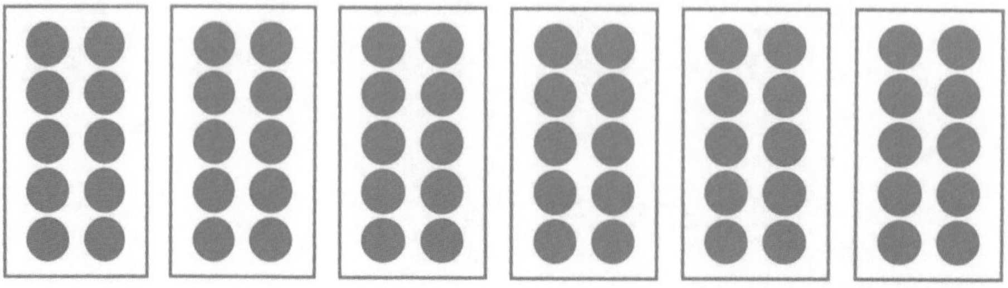

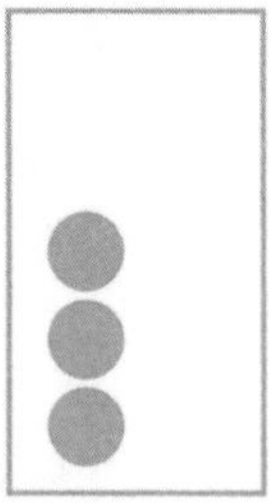

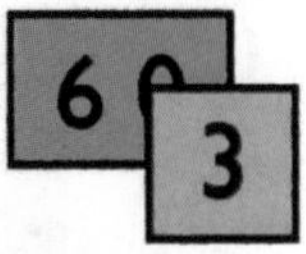

sixty-three

60 and 3 make 63.

63 = ☐ tens ☐ ones

3. Count the tens and ones.

(a)

☐ tens ☐ ones = ☐

(b)

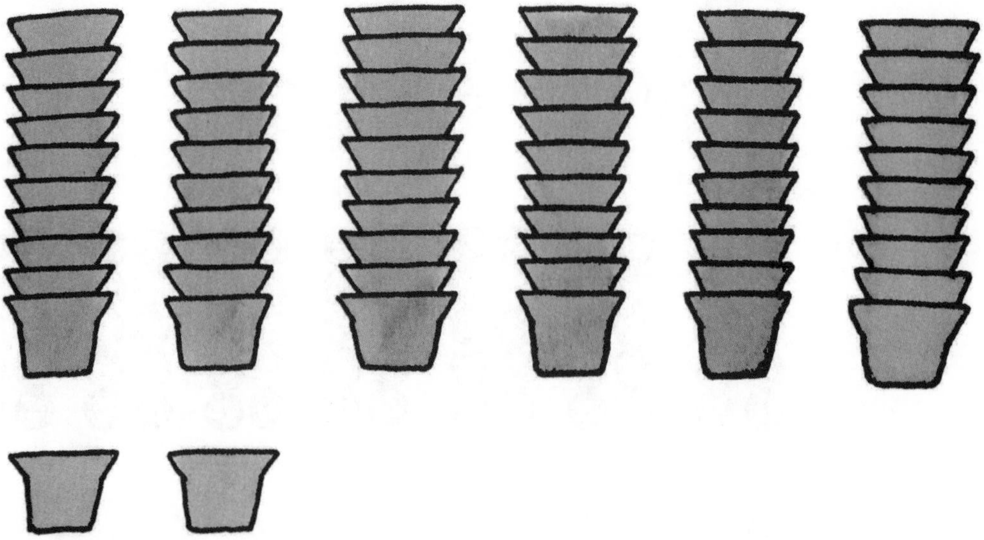

☐ tens ☐ ones = ☐

(c)

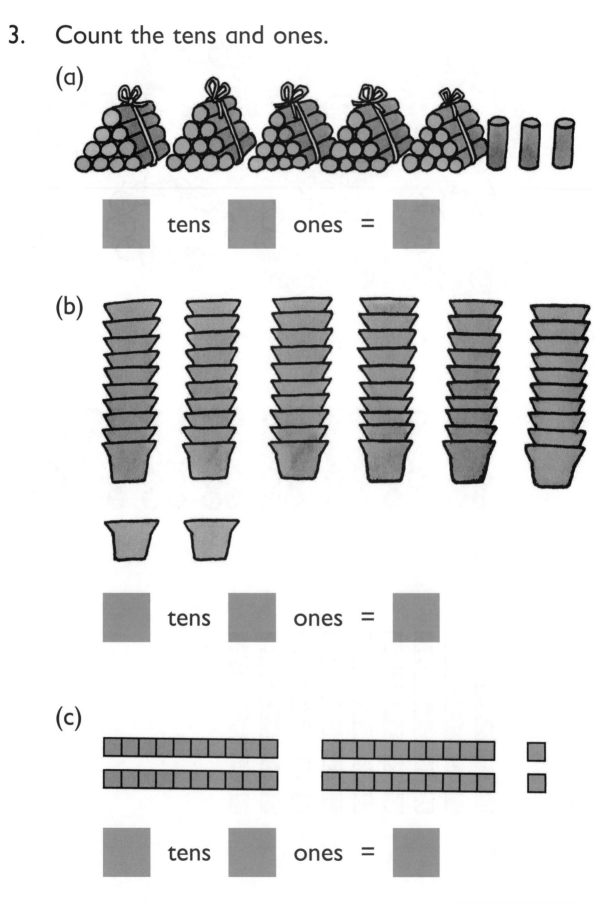

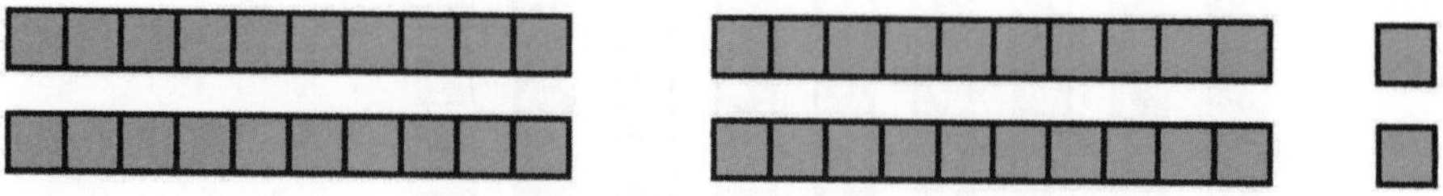

☐ tens ☐ ones = ☐

Workbook Exercises 47 to 49

4. (a)

70 + 1 = ☐

(b)

70 + ☐ = ☐

(c)

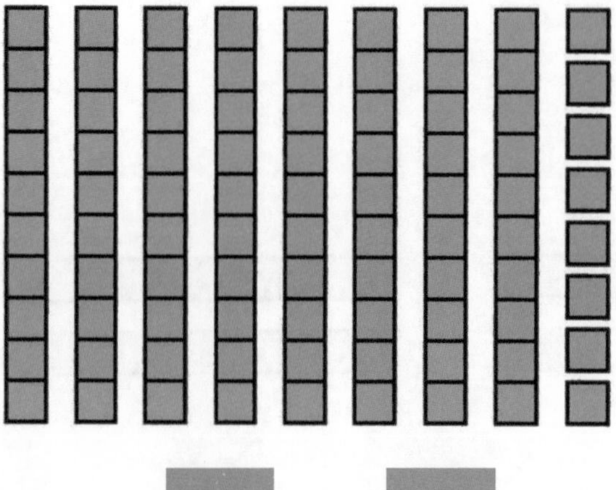

80 + ☐ = ☐

Workbook Exercise 50

2 Order of Numbers

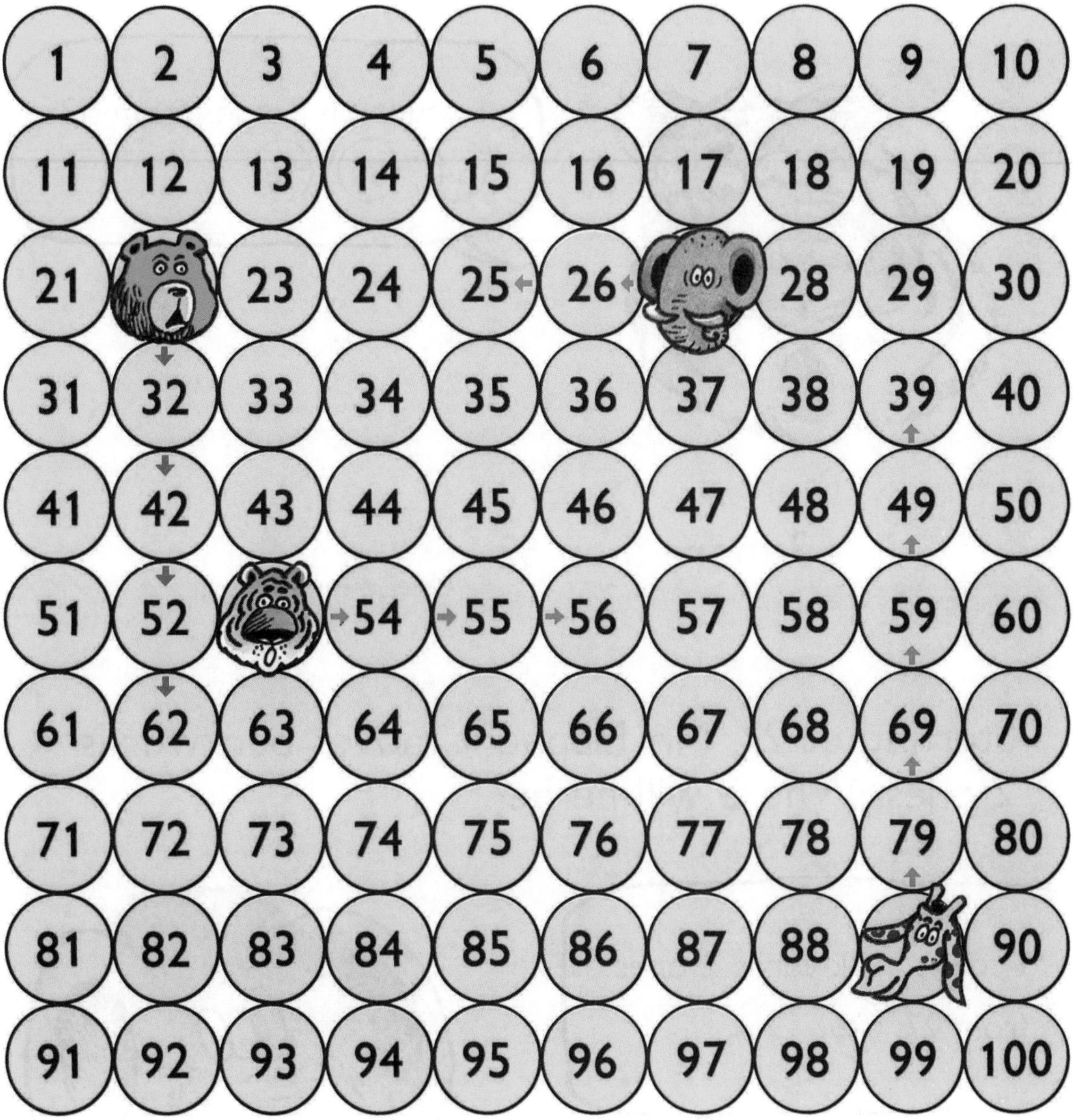

Mr. Tiger is at 53.

Where are Mr. Elephant, Mrs. Bear and Miss Giraffe?

Starting at 53, Mr. Tiger moves on 3 ones. Where will he be?

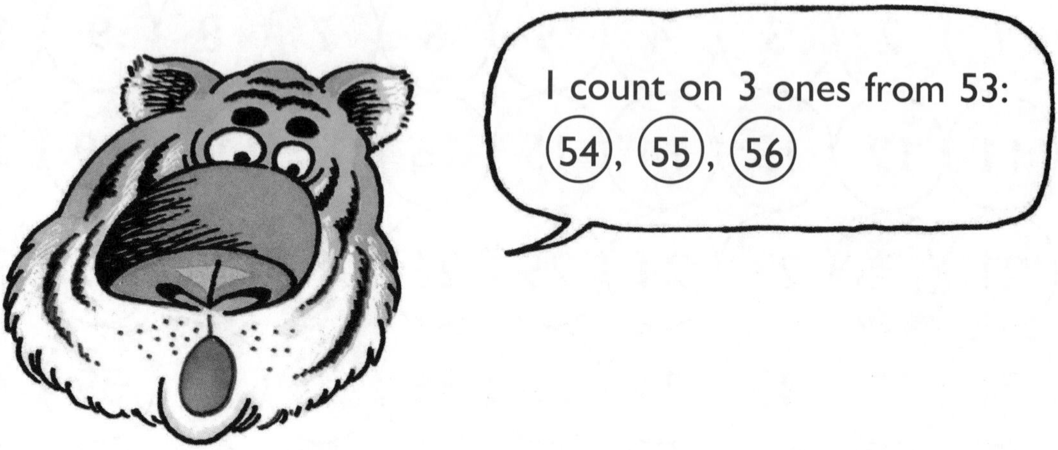
I count on 3 ones from 53:
54, 55, 56

3 more than 53 is ☐.

Starting at 27, Mr. Elephant moves backwards 2 ones. Where will he be?

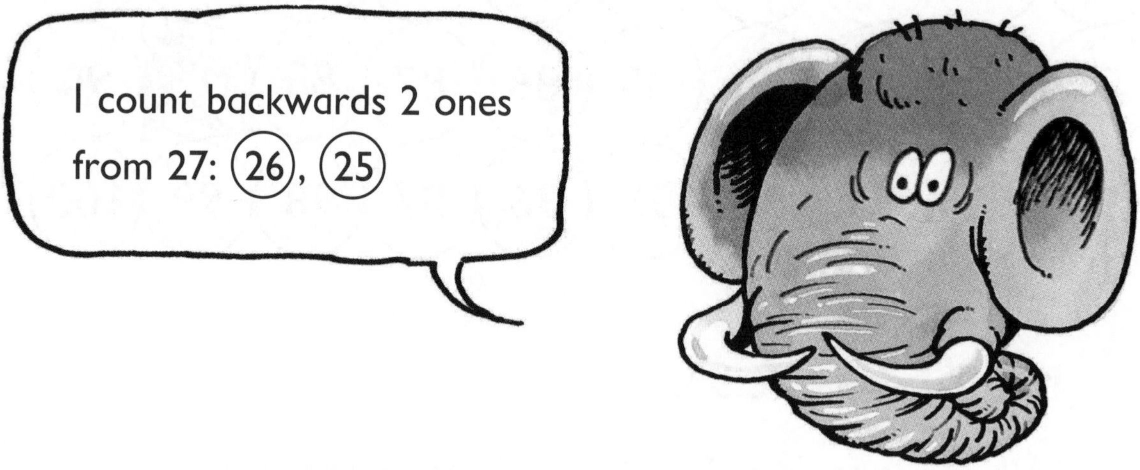
I count backwards 2 ones from 27: 26, 25

2 less than 27 is ☐.

Starting at 22, Mrs. Bear moves on 4 tens.

Where will she be?

I count on 4 tens from 22:

(32), (42), (52), (62)

40 more than 22 is ___ .

Starting at 89, Miss. Giraffe moves backwards 5 tens. Where will she be?

I count backwards 5 tens from 89:

(79), (69), (59), (49), (39)

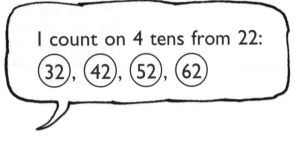

50 less than 89 is ___ .

1.

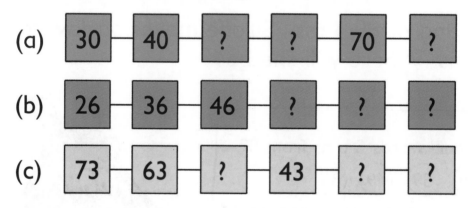

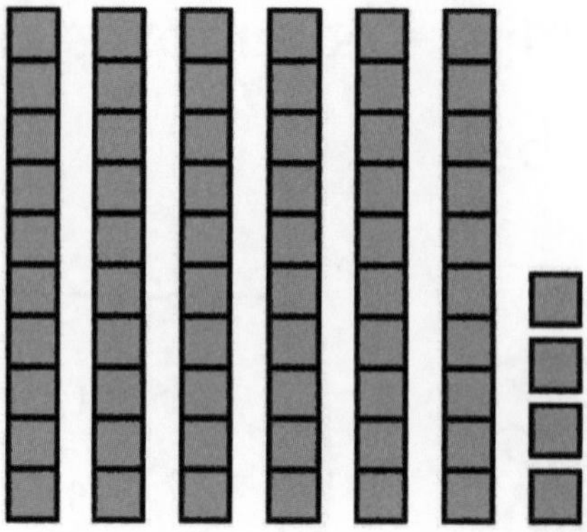

(a) What number is 1 more than 64?

(b) What number is 1 less than 64?

(c) What number is 10 more than 64?

(d) What number is 10 less than 64?

2. What are the missing numbers?

(a) 30 — 40 — ? — ? — 70 — ?

(b) 26 — 36 — 46 — ? — ? — ?

(c) 73 — 63 — ? — 43 — ? — ?

3. (a) What number is 10 more than 52?

(b) What number is 20 more than 52?

(c) What number is 10 less than 96?

(d) What number is 20 less than 96?

Workbook Exercises 51 to 56

3 Addition Within 100

Add 54 and 3.

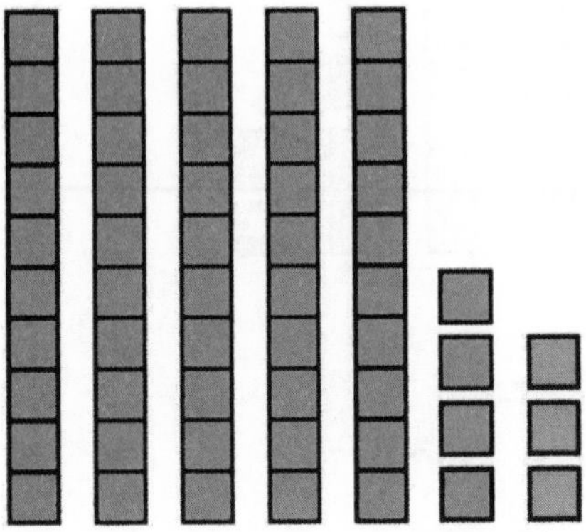

$54 + 3 = \square$

Count on 3 ones from 54:

(55), (56), (57)

$54 + 3$

50   4

Add 4 and 3.

1.

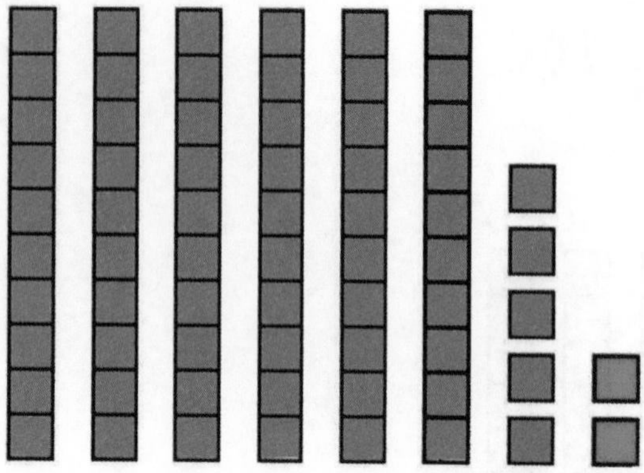

65 + 2 = ☐

Workbook Exercise 57

2. (a)

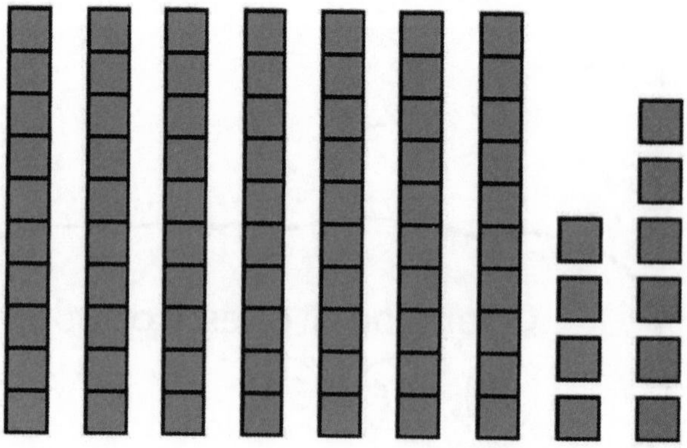

74 + 6 = ☐

(b)

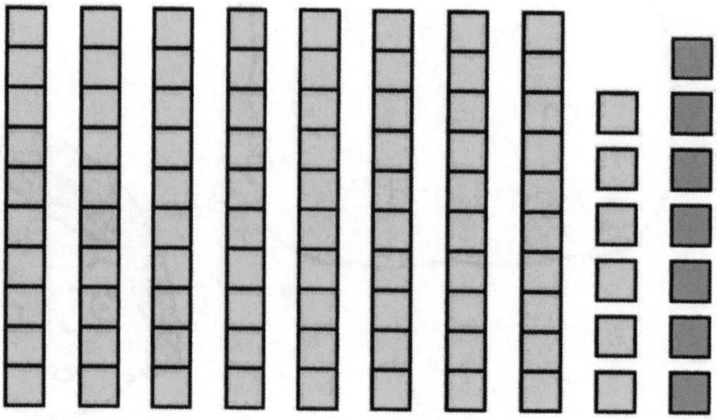

86 + 7 = ☐

Workbook Exercise 58

3. Add 62 and 30.

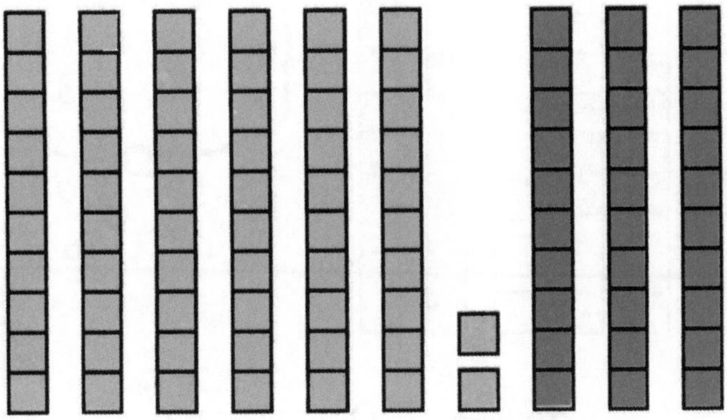

62 + 30 = ☐

Count on 3 tens from 62:
72, 82, 92

62 + 30
60 2
Add 60 and 30.

4. (a)

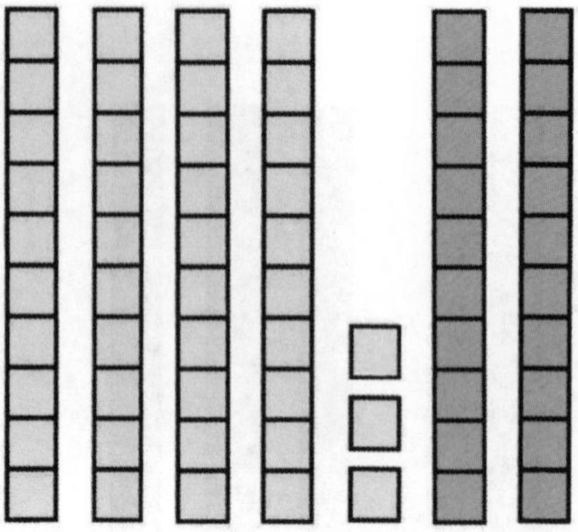

$43 + 20 =$ ▢

(b)

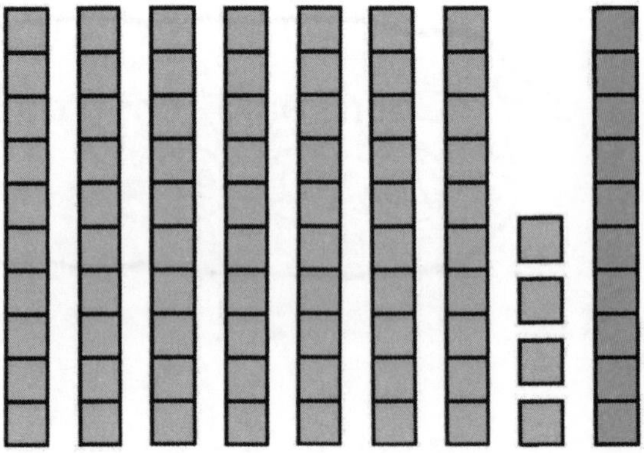

$74 + 10 =$ ▢

(c)

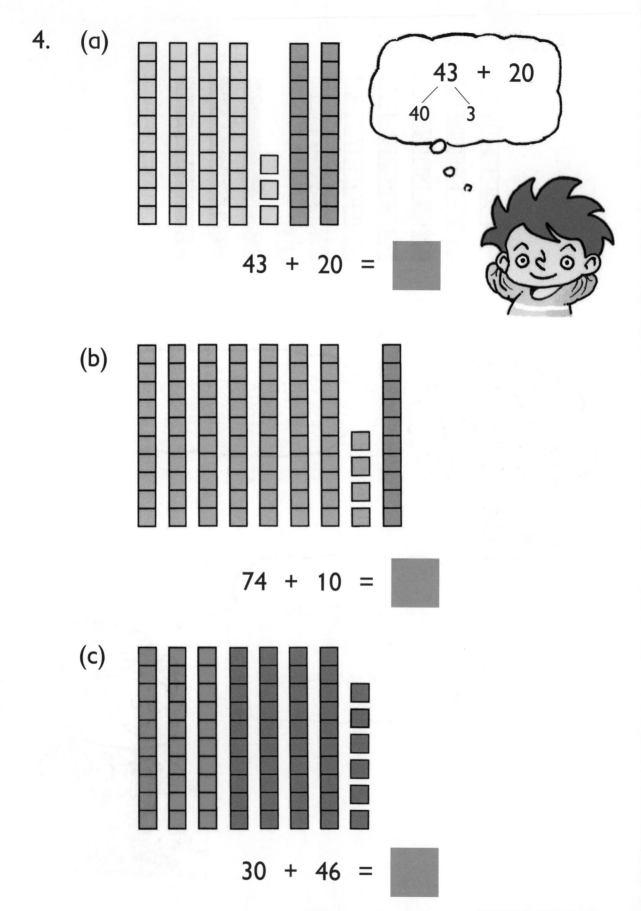

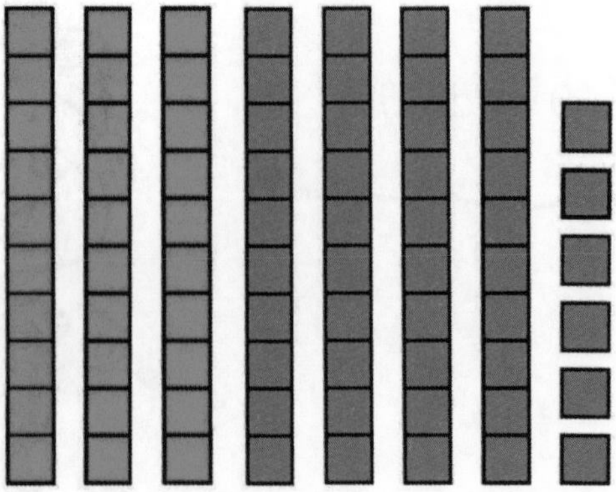

$30 + 46 =$ ▢

Workbook Exercises 59 & 60

5. Add 32 and 16.

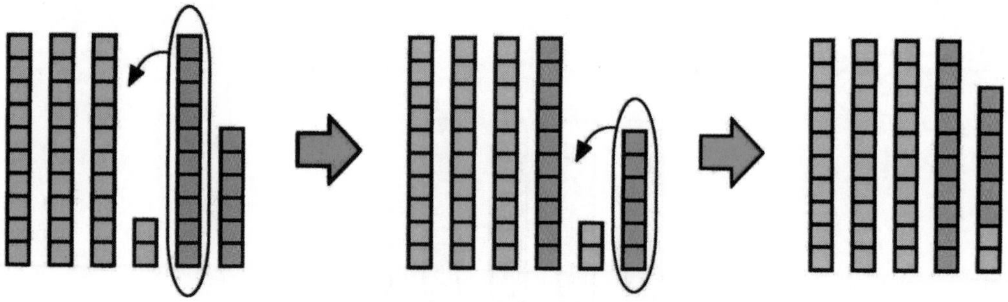

32 + 16 = ▢

6. Add 43 and 35.

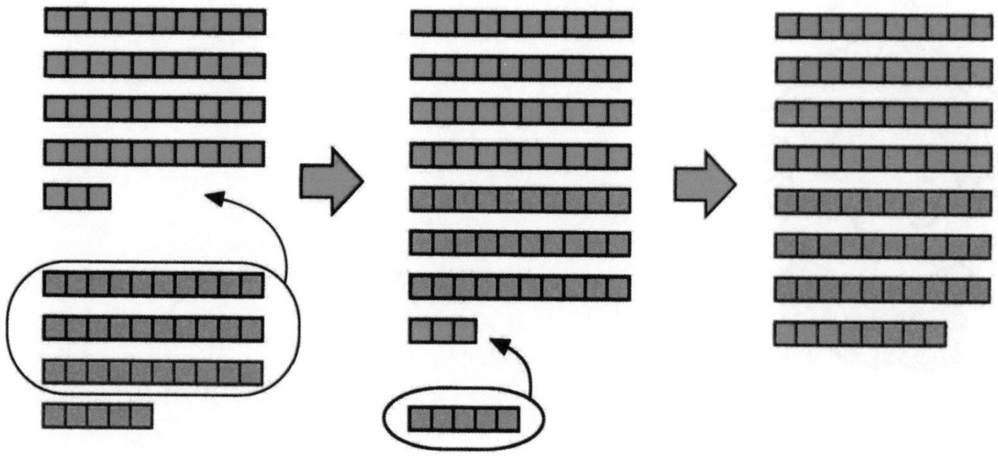

43 + 35 = ▢

Workbook Exercise 61

4 Subtraction Within 100

Subtract 2 from 48.

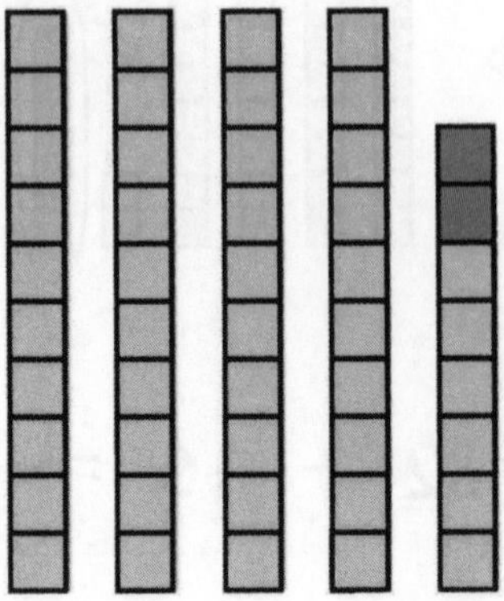

$48 - 2 = \square$

Count backwards 2 ones from 48:

(47), (46)

$48 - 2$

40 8

Subtract 2 from 8.

1. (a)

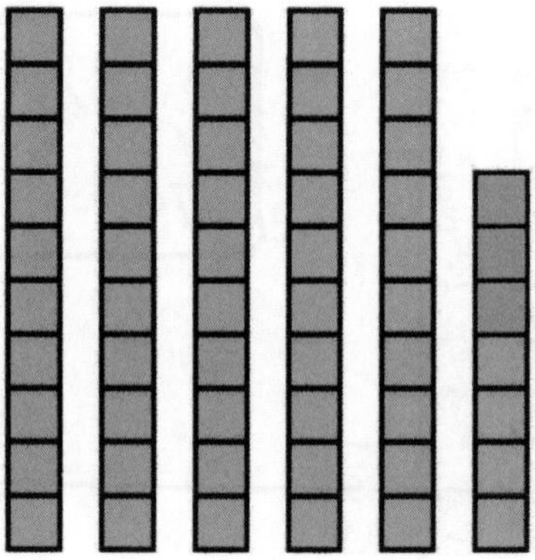

57 – 3 = ▢

(b)

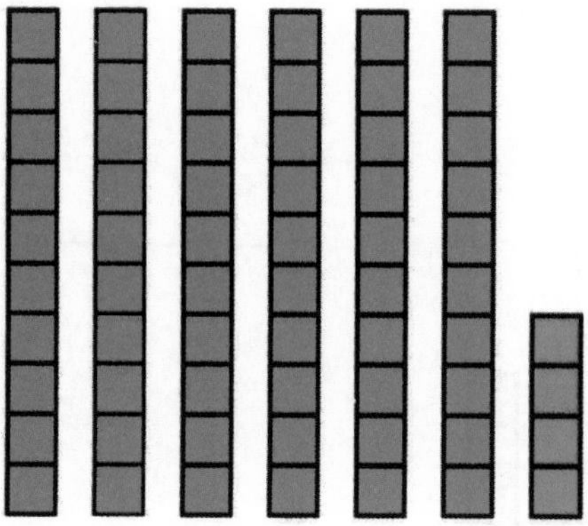

64 – 4 = ▢

Workbook Exercise 62

2. (a)

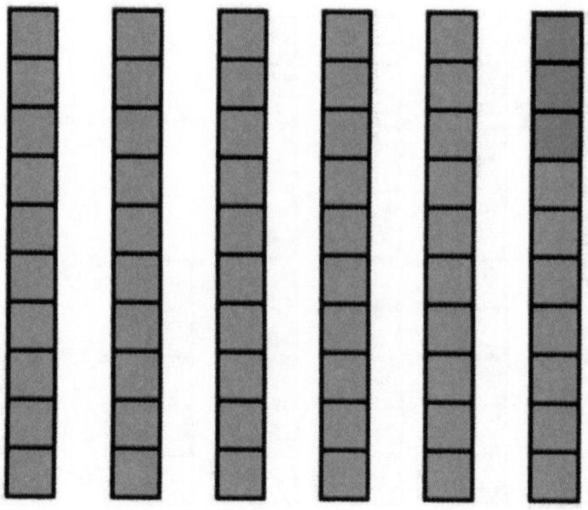

60 – 3 = ▢

(b)

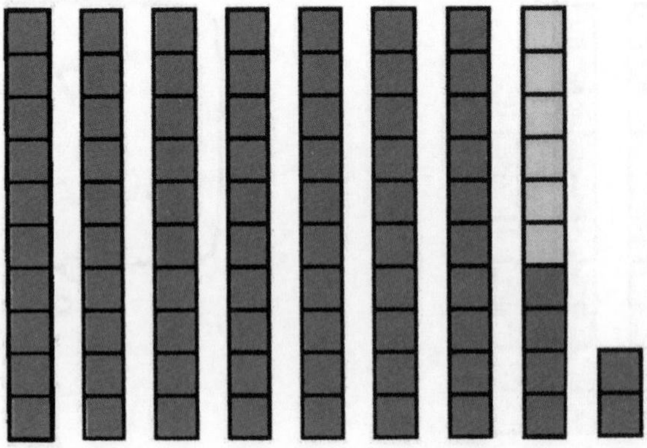

82 – 6 = ▢

(c)

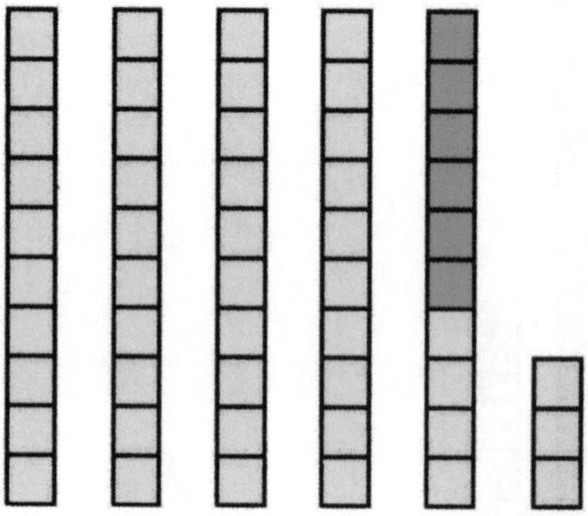

53 – 6 = ▢

(d)

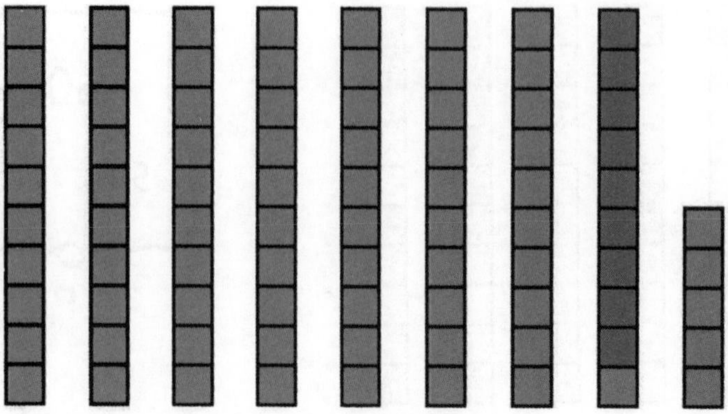

85 – 9 = ▢

Workbook Exercise 63

3. Subtract 20 from 53.

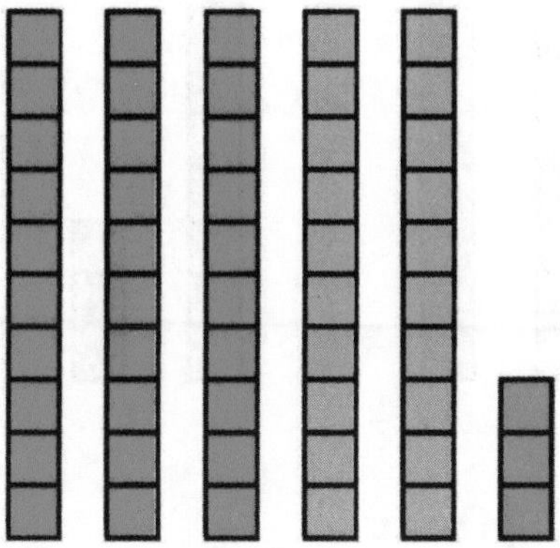

$53 - 20 = \square$

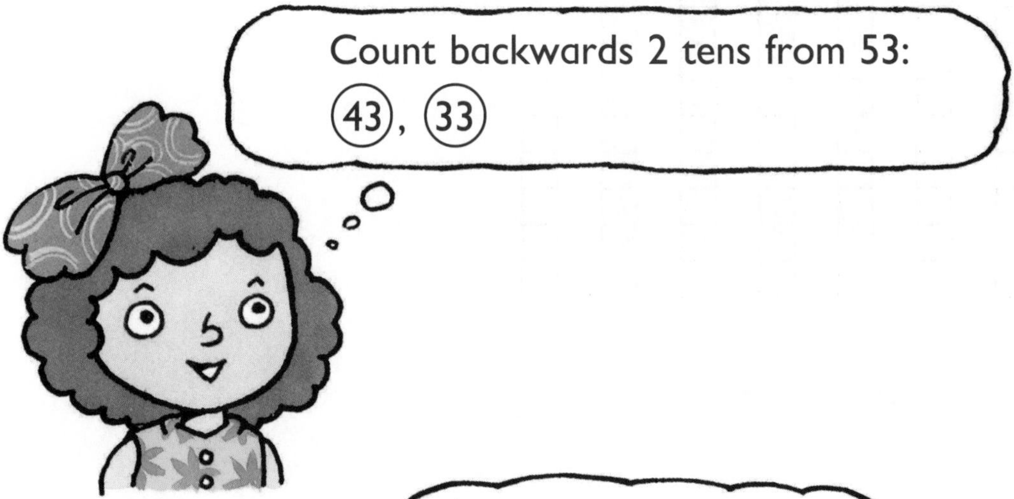
Count backwards 2 tens from 53:
43, 33

53 – 20
50 3
Subtract 20 from 50.

4. (a)

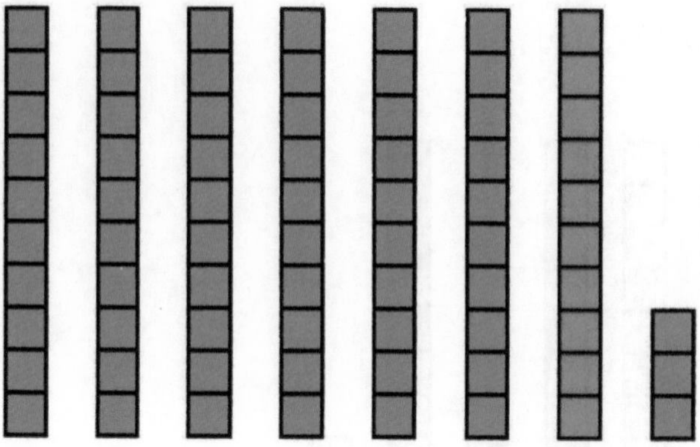

$73 - 10 = \square$

(b)

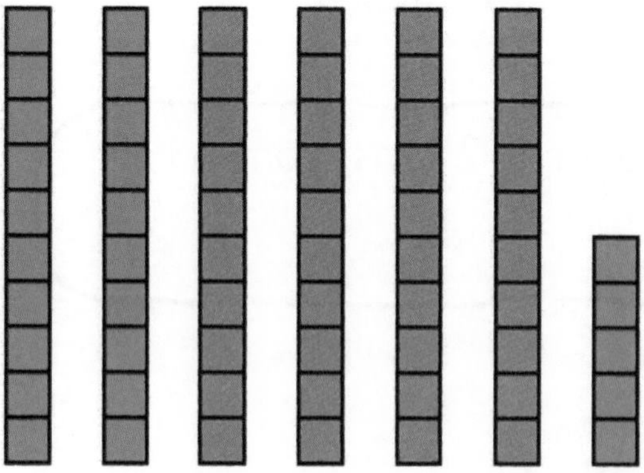

$65 - 40 = \square$

(c)

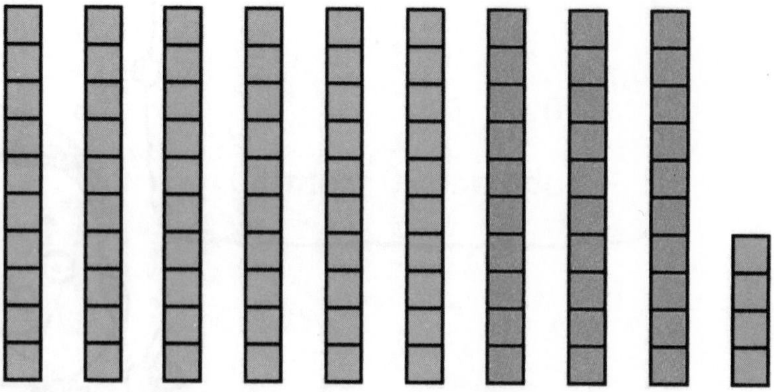

$94 - 30 = \square$

Workbook Exercises 64 & 65

5. Subtract 14 from 56.

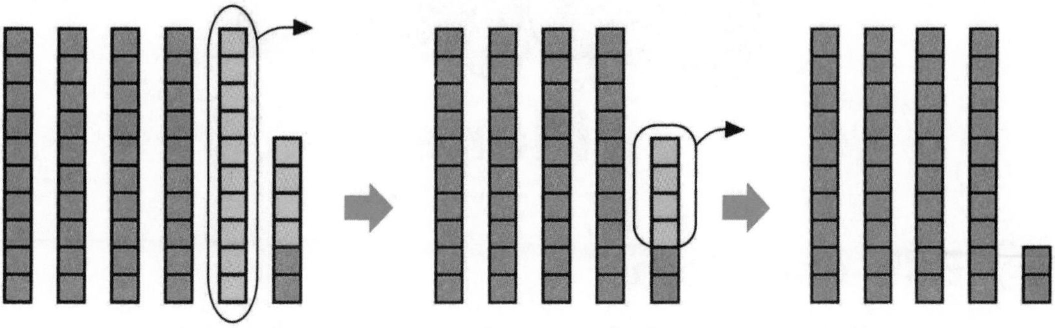

56 − 14 = ▢

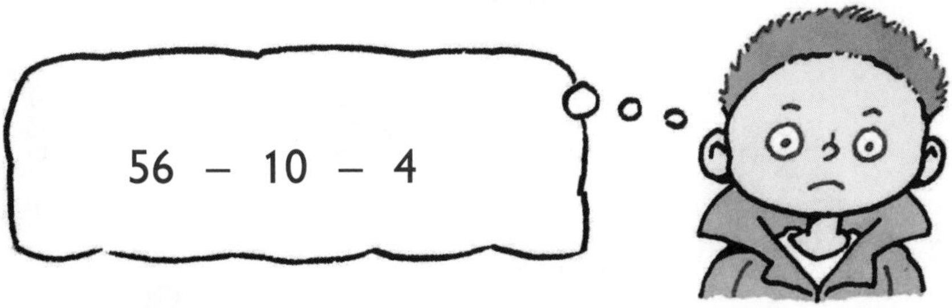

6. Subtract 32 from 78.

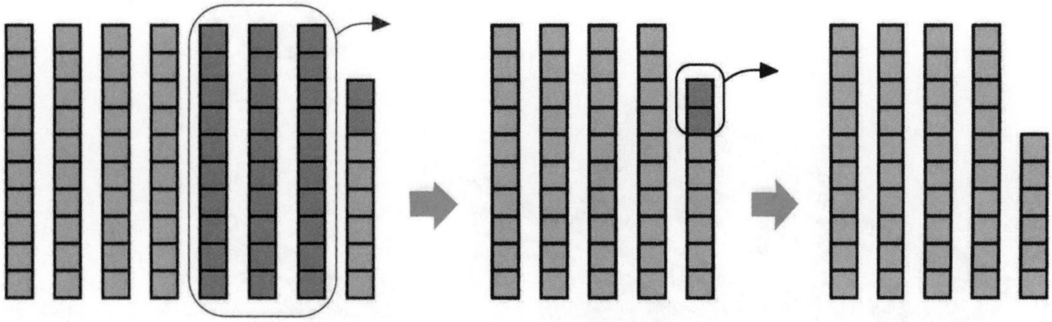

78 − 32 = ▢

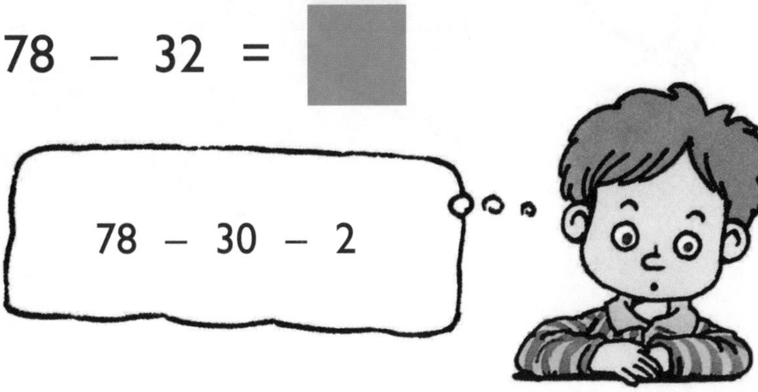

Workbook Exercise 66

9

Money

1 Bills and Coins

We use these coins and bills in the U.S.

Do you know their values?

A half-dollar can be changed for ____ dimes.

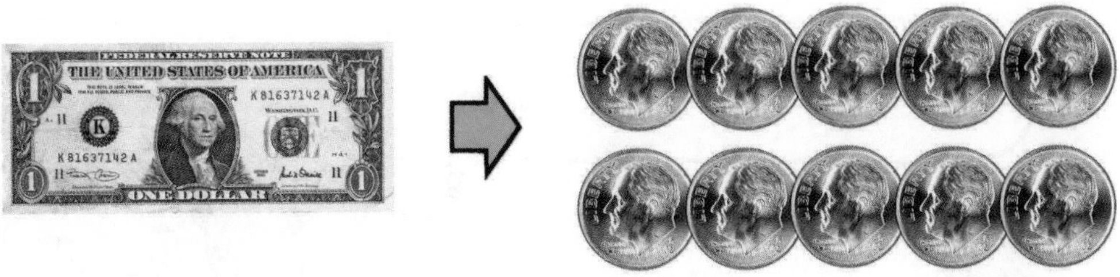

A one-dollar bill can be changed for ____ dimes.

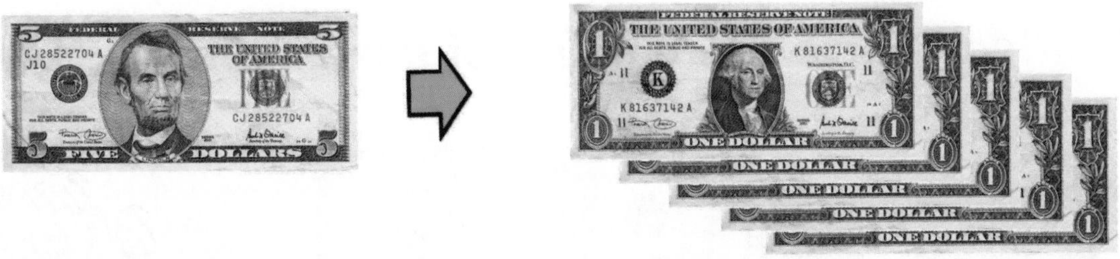

A five-dollar bill can be changed for

____ one-dollar bills.

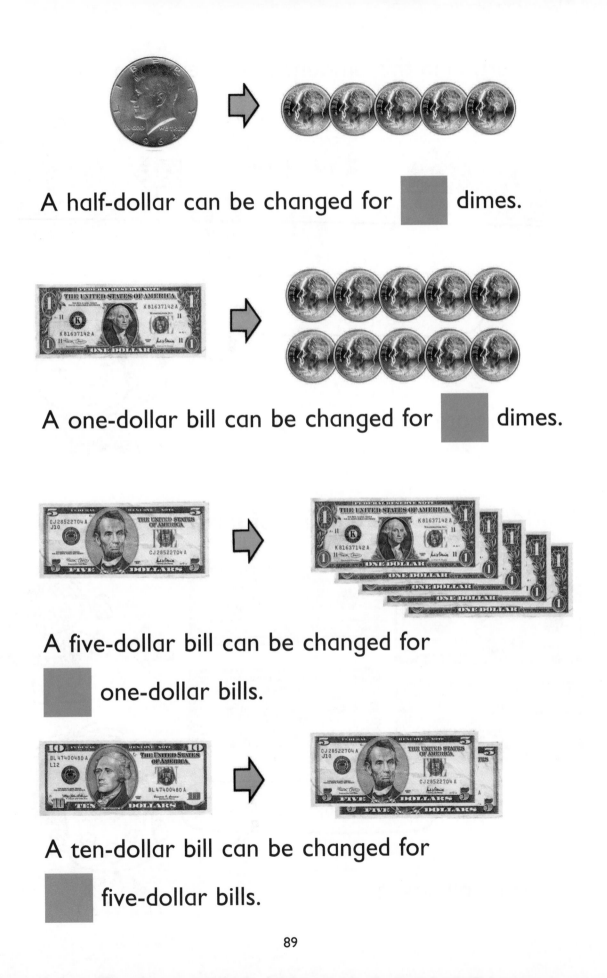

A ten-dollar bill can be changed for

____ five-dollar bills.

1. Mary paid this amount of money for a note book.

25, 50, 60, 70, 80, 90, 95 cents

The note book cost ___ ¢.

2. Maria paid this amount of money for a doll.

10, 15, 16, 17 dollars

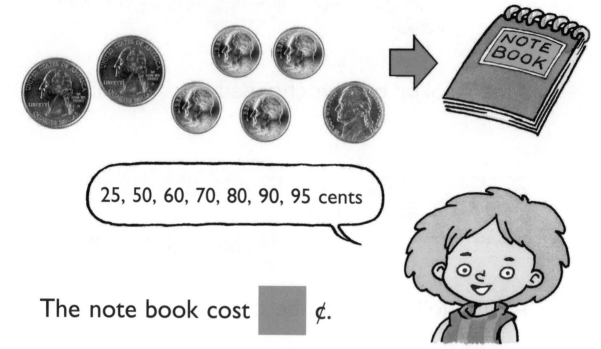

The doll cost $ ___ .

3. How much money is there in each set of coins?

(a)

(b)

(c)

(d)

(e)

(f)

Workbook Exercise 67

4. How much money is there in each set?

(a)

(b)

(c)

(d)

(e)

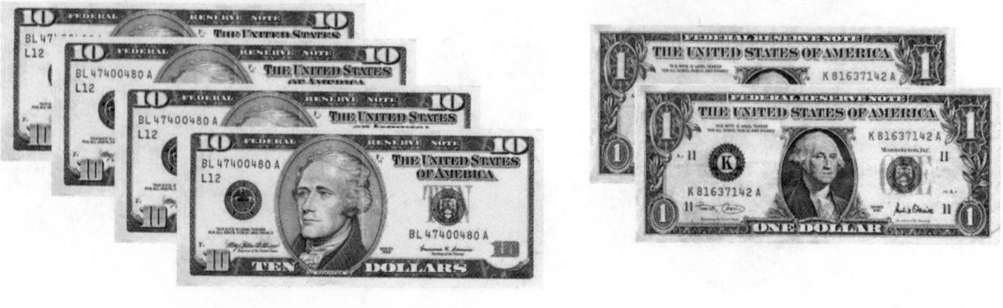

Workbook Exercise 68

5. Which set has a bigger amount of money?

(a)

Set A

Set B

(b)

Set X

Set Y

6. Which is cheaper?

(a)

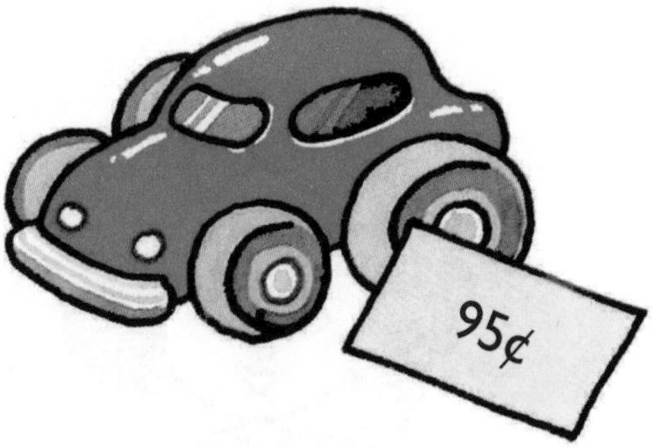

(b)

2 Shopping

$17

I have $20. I have $3 left
after buying the doll.

$20 – $17 = $3

Dani

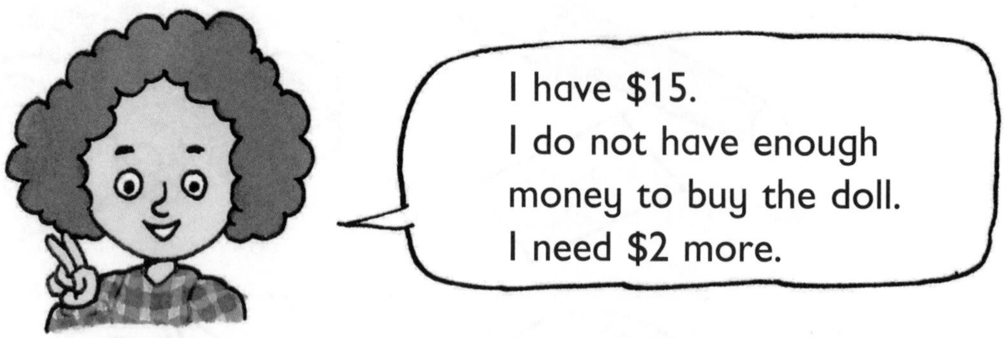
I have $15.
I do not have enough
money to buy the doll.
I need $2 more.

Emily

$17 – $15 = $2

1.

Sumin wants to buy these two things.
How much money does she need?

30¢ + 40¢ = ☐ ¢

She needs ☐ ¢.

2.

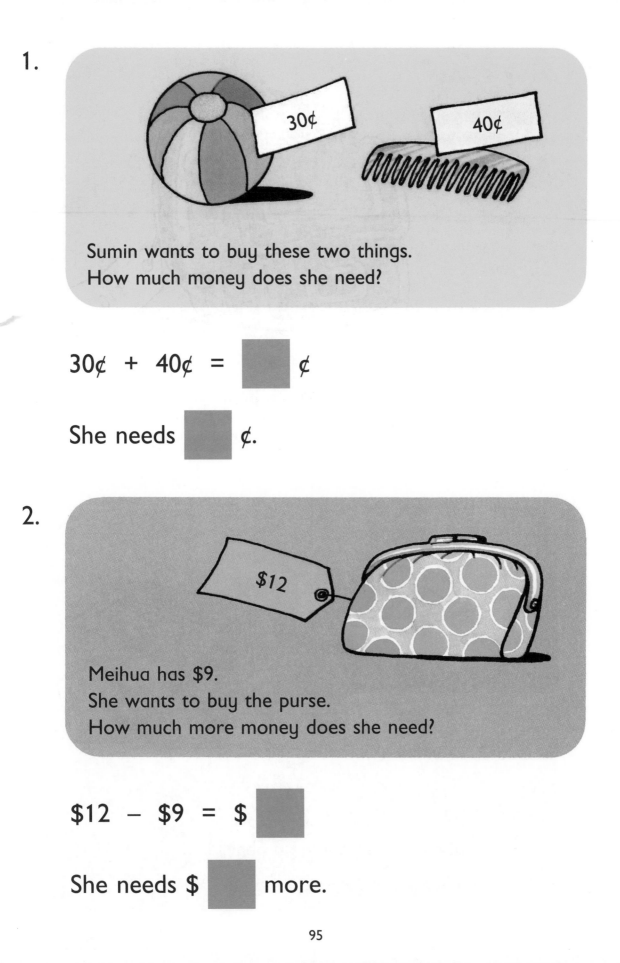

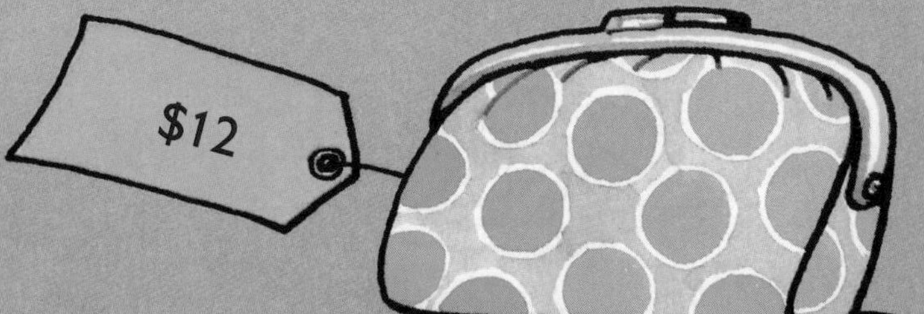

Meihua has $9.
She wants to buy the purse.
How much more money does she need?

$12 – $9 = $ ☐

She needs $ ☐ more.

3.

Ali had $2 left after buying the bag.
How much did he have at first?

4.

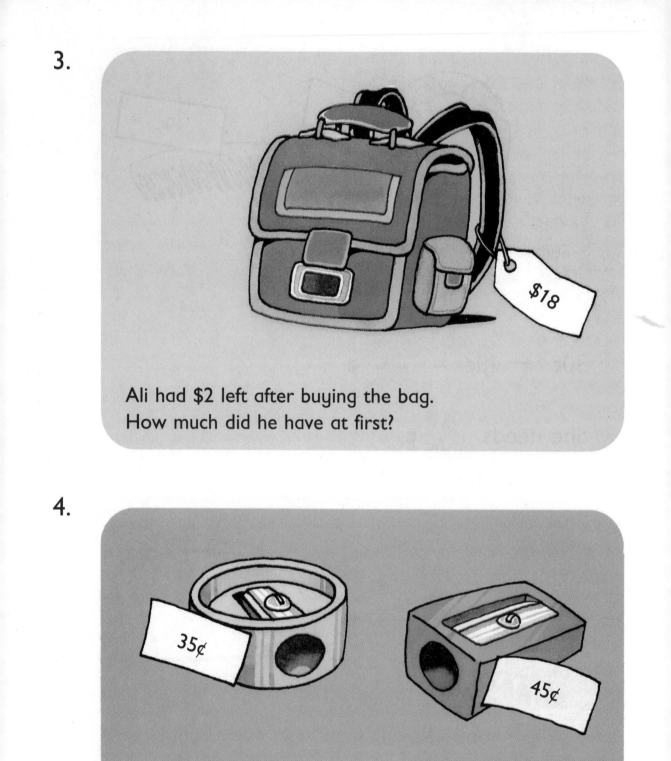

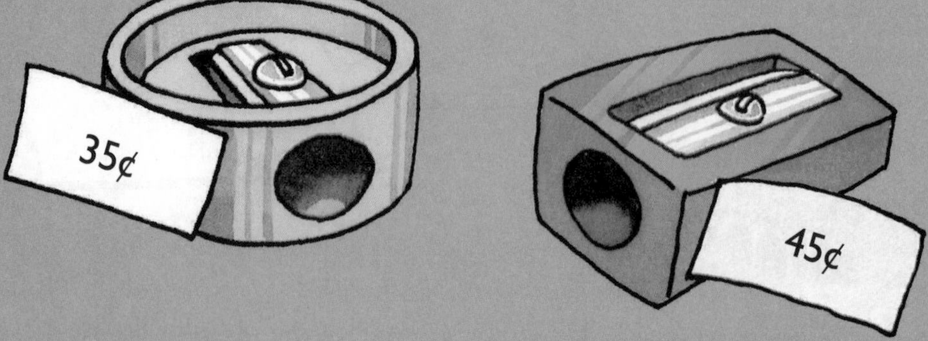

Raju had $1.

He had 65¢ left after buying a pencil sharpener.

Which pencil sharpener did he buy?

Workbook Exercise 70